Anatomy of Breathing

Anatomy of Breathing

Text and illustrations by
Blandine Calais-Germain

French edition published in 2005 by Éditions DésIris as
Respiration: anatomie – geste respiratoire.

English edition ©2006 by Éditions DésIris
Cover illustration ©2006 by Julie Paschkis

Published by Eastland Press, Inc.
P.O. Box 99749
Seattle, WA 98139, USA
www.eastlandpress.com

Library of Congress Control Number: 2006929335
ISBN-13: 978-0-939616-55-8
ISBN-10: 0-939616-55-6

4 6 8 10 9 7 5

Translated by Regine MacKenzie
Edited by Allan Kaplan and John O'Connor

Book design by Gary Niemeier

Table of Contents

Table of Contents

Acknowledgements

All my thanks to…

Jean-Bernard Arbeit
Pau, Uriel, Mateu Bruguera
Félix Castellano
Bernard Coignard
Joséphine Contreras
Anne-Marie Doe de Maindreville
François Doe de Maindreville
Catherine Feuillet
Barbara Gaultier
François Gibut
Brigitte Hap
Francis Jeser
Christiane Mangiapani
Jose Luis marin Mateo
Patricia Romero
Frédéric Sauvage
Michel Sanchez
Nuria Vives
Sophie Zufferey

…who have helped by posing for the illustrations, proofreading the text, and sticking with me on a daily basis through my writing and drawing.

Foreword

MORE THAN TEN years ago, the first Spanish edition of *Anatomy of Movement* by Blandine Calais Germain was published. Year after year, new printings were published and new books by Blandine appeared. These added up to a remarkable volume of information for all people interested in movement, and particularly students of the theory and practice of movement.

In her latest work, *Anatomy of Breathing*, Blandine studies the thoracic cage, the airway passages, the organs and muscles involved in respiration while focusing special attention on the diaphragm and the physiology of respiratory volumes. She analyzes respiratory movement in all its anatomical aspects, considering both the internal and external forces involved. She also looks at the principal types of respiratory movement and their phases, describing approximately thirty different types of respiratory activity.

This book is filled with beautiful illustrations drawn by the author herself. They reveal her capacity to communicate with great sensitivity all the complex sensations involved in respiratory movement. We have observed this sensitivity in her courses, which she offers to physiotherapists at our university in Valencia.

This is truly an innovative book that is very important for reference purposes and very useful for practical applications. This book should be a part of the library of every student and professional interested in the study of respiratory kinetics and their application in the fields of physical therapy, rehabilitation, physical education, psychology, sports, and the performing arts.

Manuel A. Valls Barbera
Former Department Head, Centre Hospitalier Universitaire La Fe
Professor, Department of Physical Therapy, University of Valencia (Spain)

Preface

FROM THE TIME I first became a dance teacher, I started observing and studying breathing and how to use it in a coordinated manner. It played an important role in practice and in the lessons I gave at the Ecole Anne-Marie Debatte, the creative dance studio where I taught. I observed its influence on the functioning and expressiveness of movement.

I became increasingly aware of variations in the act of breathing as it occurs in the individual, and as it coexists as a counterpoint to the other movements of the body: sometimes the two movements are superimposed, sometimes they become independent of each other, and sometimes one causes the other and vice versa.

This experience was enriched by scientific discoveries during my study of physiotherapy, and by many questions and answers over the course of that study, especially with respect to vocal technique. It became apparent to me that breathing was one of the most misunderstood aspects of bodywork, with a lot of mistaken ideas floating around. For example, a number of people believe that the lungs open the rib cage by expanding, that the diaphragm rises during inhalation, and that it even pulls the organs upward. Almost everyone thinks of inhalation as an upward movement.

In this field, there are also a lot of existing rules among the various forms of bodywork, rules that are not grounded in much evidence. For example, some say that it is better to inhale than to exhale, while others say just the opposite. Recently, I heard a television program teach us "how to breathe well by breathing through the belly rather than the thorax, since that makes the air circulate better." Elsewhere there is a belief that you must absolutely develop rib breathing, and so forth. I have found none of these breathing techniques to be harmful per se, but I have also found that none of them is the only correct way. You must choose with care.

My hope is that these observations, and the book that resulted from them, will contribute to a more enlightened practice of breathing. I also hope that you, the reader, will have a better understanding of how breathing changes spontaneously from moment to moment. My other wish is that you will discover how to consciously choose a specific breathing technique for certain purposes or circumstances.

This book is intended to help you understand the act of breathing, both in theory and practice.

THEORY

- You will see how breathing happens, and how it varies.

- You will become acquainted with the principal structures involved in the movements of breathing. This is the anatomical side.

- You will learn to recognize the forces involved in breathing and how they influence the way each movement is performed in a specific fashion. Some of these are physiological forces, and will be discussed in the anatomy section, others are external to the body.

PRACTICE

- You will do physical exercises that help prepare your body for certain types of breathing.

- You will learn to practice a few of the most common breathing techniques.

....

CHAPTER ONE

Initial Observations About the Act of Breathing

BREATHING IS THE movement that is performed in respiration. This may seem obvious, but it is largely a hidden movement which is so intimately linked to our lives that we often don't even recognize it, especially since it blends in with other movements like walking, talking, or eating.

We are completely unaware of many of the rhythmic movements that occur in our bodies: the rhythms of digestion, waking and sleeping, blood circulation, and lymphatic circulation, to name a few. Breathing is just like that. It occurs on the level of the internal organs, just like the beating of the heart; but in contrast to the heart, it also involves muscles, certain parts of the skeleton, and joint articulations. It cannot be separated from these. Breathing thus becomes an interface between two levels: the level of the organs and the level of movement. It can therefore be controlled, albeit with limitations, by the nervous system's management of either one of these two levels.

The act of breathing also permits interaction between these two levels. On the one hand, it is mostly unconscious and automatic. It influences our actions and our emotions and at the same time is influenced by them. On the other hand, it is an action that one can influence in a conscious, voluntary manner, by changing it in various ways, with consequences on many different levels.

In the first part of this book, we will look at how breathing progresses, its stages, the parts of the body that are involved, its volume, and its rate.

First of all, we should distinguish among the different meanings of the word *respiration*.

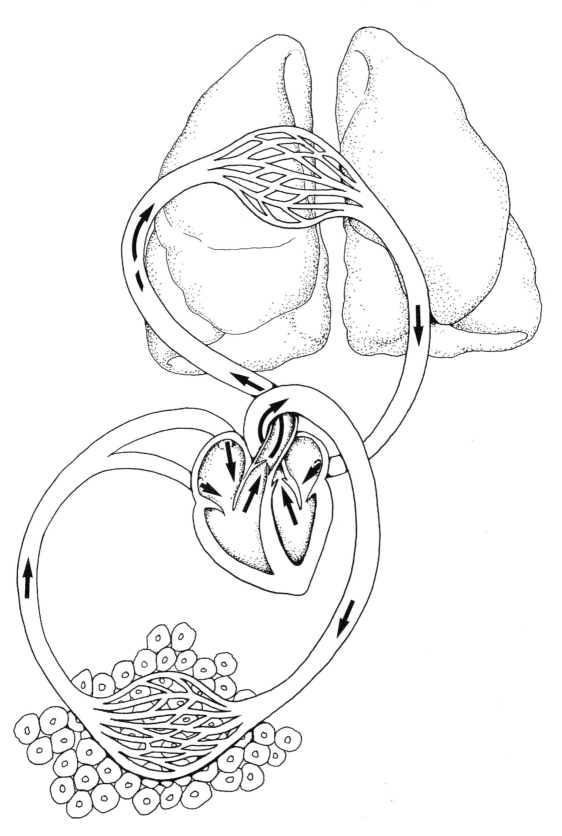

INTERNAL RESPIRATION — EXTERNAL RESPIRATION (BREATHING)

The unchanging and constant goal of respiration is the *oxygenation of the blood.*

The cells in the tissues need oxygen to function properly, and it is brought to them via the arterial blood, which comes from the lungs and the heart. This mechanism produces a waste product, carbon dioxide, which is carried in the venous blood back to the heart and the lungs.

This phenomenon is called *internal respiration.* It occurs at the tissue and cellular level.

Internal respiration is made possible by transforming venous blood into arterial blood, which occurs in the lungs. This is where oxygen and carbon dioxide are exchanged:

- From the outside, air rich in oxygen enters the lungs.

- From the tissues, blood rich in carbon dioxide arrives in the lungs.

The exchange of gases is accomplished through alveolar capillary membranes (see page 60).

Air enters the body from the outside through the lungs and leaves it again at a rate of about 12 to 15 times per minute. This phenomenon is called *external respiration,* or simply *breathing.* It occurs at the level of the lungs.

This book focuses on the movements that enable external respiration or breathing in its many variations.

The relationship between respiration and breathing

Since oxygen cannot be stored in the body, respiration is required without cease, day and night. However, the act of breathing does not always strictly depend on the oxygen needs of the body. Why? Because breathing may also serve other purposes, and be dependent on other circumstances.

Several examples will make this clear.
You can modify your breathing:

- to accompany another action

- to change emotions

- to change the body tension, either toward more relaxation or more tension

- to accompany or modify sensations of pleasure or pain

- to help the speaking or singing voice carry better

- to activate the organs

- to more forcefully open or close the rib cage

- to accentuate or moderate the curvature of the spine.

Obviously, all of these goals are not directly related to the oxygenation of the blood.

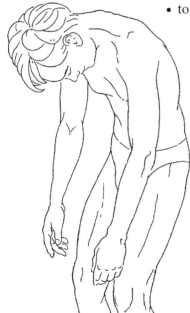

Many of these activities can occur at the same time. For example, one can inhale simultaneously to oxygenate the blood, play the flute, and sustain a musical note.

Thus there is a gap, which is more or less conscious and voluntary, between the need for oxygenation and the act of breathing.

On the other hand, you can practice breathing *without* the passage of air. This may lead to pressure differences between the thorax and the abdomen, which will be addressed in Chapter 7.

"Learning" to breathe?

You have heard it said that we don't need to learn how to breathe; it just "happens." Thus, in some activities (even very complex ones) there may be a total lack of breath training because "only spontaneous breathing will harmonize well with the movement." Yet in other activities (e.g., yoga) the breathing itself is the object of the entire learning process.

Of course, the oxygenation aspect of breathing occurs automatically and does not need to be learned. You can engage in physical activities and still maintain spontaneous breathing.

But outside of the immediate need for oxygen, there is a wide variety of breathing techniques, a rich repertoire of actions that are not always spontaneous. Most of the great bodywork traditions follow very particular ways of breathing, which are passed down through the generations.

These variations in breathing techniques are the subject of this book. They are not bound to any particular tradition, but will be studied on their own merits; they can be found in all sorts of situations.

You will find as you read through these pages that you can breathe the same amount of air in a number of different ways. You will also find that you can use different ways of breathing for purposes other than just capturing air.

BREATHING: AT FIRST GLANCE, ALWAYS THE SAME MOVEMENT

It seems as if each spontaneous breath resembles another. However, when you watch or listen to somebody breathe, or when you watch or feel your own breathing in different situations, you will note that the act of breathing changes constantly.

- It can build up in different parts of the trunk, for instance, in the ribs or in the abdomen, even though the air always enters through the lungs.

- It can affect parts of the body that are located far from the trunk.

- It can be very minimal, almost imperceptible, or big, with considerable amplitude and power.

- It can change its speed and/or rhythm.

- It can be voluntary or involuntary, changing from active to passive and back again.

- It can be quiet or loud.

Yet all breathing has one thing in common: It consists of a constant movement (coming and going) of air via *inhalation* and *exhalation*, interrupted by a cessation of breathing, which is called *apnea*.

We will start our study of breathing with these movements.

Inhalation

You breathe in air, without ceasing, at an average rate of 12 to 15 times per minute.

Inhalation is the process of taking air from outside the body into your lungs. In some of the illustrations in this book, this process is represented by an arrow which depicts the movement of air into the body.

During this process, some part of your trunk, either the abdomen or the ribs, will expand.

- Inhalation can occur with different amplitudes or volumes of air. You can breathe in more air or less air (see pages 25-29).

- It occurs at variable rates. You can breathe in faster or slower, accelerating or slowing down the act of breathing.

- It can be more or less loud.

- It can be less active — during relaxation — or more active, and more forceful — for example, while taking in a big gulp of air. Certain forms of breathing can be completely passive (see pages 113 and 117). Some relaxation techniques use this type of breathing.

- Inhalation may occur more at the level of the rib cage or at the abdomen.

- It may also occur more towards the front or the back of the trunk.

Exhalation

Exhalation is the process of letting air flow from the lungs back to the outside of the body. In some of the illustrations in this book, this process is represented by an arrow which depicts the movement of air flowing out of the body.

Often, exhalation is accompanied by a bending or closing of parts of the trunk, either the ribs, the belly, or the spinal column.

- Like inhalation, exhalation can occur with very different amplitudes or volumes of air, that is, you can empty your lungs more or less completely (see pages 26-28).

- It can also occur at different rates. You can breathe out faster or more slowly, accelerating or slowing down the act of breathing.

- Exhalation can occur with or without sound, sometimes linked to a specific intention, for example, when you speak or sing.

- Exhalation is usually passive during relaxed breathing. But it can become active or very forceful, for example, when exhaling a lot of air.

- The act of exhaling may occur more at the level of the ribs (by dropping the ribs) or of the abdomen (by raising the belly upwards).

- It may also occur more towards the front or the back of the trunk.

Apnea (cessation of breathing)

Apnea (from the Greek word *a-pnein*: *a* – without, *pnein* – breathing) describes every moment where the *flow of air is absent.*

This cessation can occur at any time during breathing.

It often manifests at the level of the thorax by a suspension of movement.

During normal breathing, this cessation occurs naturally, when the act of breathing reverses itself:

- After inhalation, there is a short pause where you stop breathing before you exhale.

- After exhalation, there is often a longer pause without breathing before you again inhale.

- Generally, the physiological apneas are of regular duration and occur automatically, depending on the body's need for oxygen or the need to get rid of carbon dioxide.

But you can also consciously and voluntarily change the duration of the apnea, shortening or prolonging it. (This is often used in physical activities.)

However, you can't stop breathing indefinitely. When the body has reached its physical limits, it will automatically resume breathing.

Cessation of breathing may occur at a relaxed moment (after a relaxed exhalation), or a very active moment (e.g., when you try to hold your breath as long as possible after a very big inhalation).

Finally, it should be noted that the cessation of breathing may occur at the level of the rib cage (high breathing) or of the abdomen (low breathing).

Breathing can cause movement in any part of the trunk, but the air goes only into the lungs

Whether it is costal or abdominal breathing, the act of breathing can affect almost all regions of the trunk. Thus, you can inhale or exhale while feeling movement, for example:

- at the front of the ribs, but also at the back or on the sides

- higher or lower in the rib cage

- around the waist

- at the front of the abdomen (at different levels)

- further down in the region of the pelvis, either in the front or back, or in the perineum.

This is why we talk about breathing into your belly, into the clavicles, the back, and so forth. Of course, the inhaled air does not actually reach all parts of the body that are moved during breathing; even when you inhale very deeply, the air never goes anywhere but to the lungs, which occupy only a small portion of the thorax.

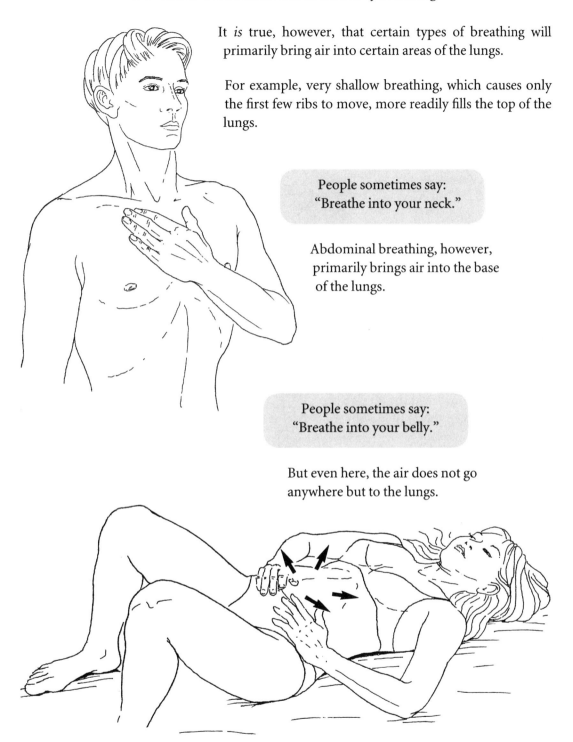

It *is* true, however, that certain types of breathing will primarily bring air into certain areas of the lungs.

For example, very shallow breathing, which causes only the first few ribs to move, more readily fills the top of the lungs.

People sometimes say:
"Breathe into your neck."

Abdominal breathing, however, primarily brings air into the base of the lungs.

People sometimes say:
"Breathe into your belly."

But even here, the air does not go anywhere but to the lungs.

That is why it is important not to confuse the location where the airflow occurs, which is always in the lungs, with the locations where movement is felt in the trunk, because of the act of breathing itself or the type of breathing that is used.

TWO TYPES OF BREATHING

There are two principal types of breathing:

- *Costal breathing*:
  This is breathing that works with the ribs. It opens them during inhalation and closes them during exhalation.

- *Diaphragmatic breathing*:
  This is breathing that works with the abdominal area. It causes the abdomen to bulge during inhalation and draws it back in during exhalation.

These two types of breathing involve two completely different ways of moving the lungs.

You can mix and match them in different ways, and thereby create many variations of breathing. But, as you will see over the course of this work, in the end all of these variations come back to one or the other principal type of breathing.

Contrary to what is sometimes taught, none of these variations in breathing is the only good one, and none of them is really bad. They just fit different circumstances and can be used for different purposes. Therefore, it is important to practice a variety of breathing techniques, especially when you realize that you have a tendency to use one technique all the time.

RESPIRATORY VOLUMES

During both inhalation and exhalation, breathing occurs with different amplitudes, which is to say, different volumes of air.

In practice, the volume of airflow through the lungs is never the same from one breath to the next. This is due to variations in activity and thus to different demands for oxygen. The most regular volume exchange occurs while sleeping. Apart from that, we can identify several characteristic volumes.

It is important to clearly distinguish among different types of volume, and to recognize them as they occur in a particular physical exercise. Why? Because the mechanics of breathing are very different for each volume, the effects will be different too.

Now, we often string together or combine different types of volume, even within the same breath, without being aware of it; this makes it hard to interpret what is actually happening. It is therefore a good idea to have a clear understanding of what a volume is, first by identifying each individual volume, and then by recognizing them in the course of several breaths strung together.

Later, you will find out which forces play a role within each respiratory volume. This is described on pages 117-124.

In the end, you will understand how all these details work together during the execution of a breath. This is basic information that will help you adapt your breathing in real time to perform a specific movement or achieve a certain goal. That is why in the course of this book I refer frequently to the notion of volume.

Tidal volume: "normal" breathing

When you are at rest, or performing an activity that is not very strenuous (e.g., reading), you breathe with little amplitude. This is the most common type of breathing. Here you exchange about a half liter of air per breath. The precise volume depends on the physique of the person, more for a heavy adult and less for a child.

In practice, tidal volume varies a bit, depending on the circumstances. During deep relaxation or sleep, it is at its minimum. During moderate activity, for example, a short walk at a relaxed pace, you breathe a little more air. But this is still the tidal volume. We will see on pages 118 and 119 that this volume is characterized by the forces brought into play.

Both inhalation and exhalation can be performed with this volume of "normal" breathing. At any point during inhalation or exhalation, you can also stop breathing (apnea).

In practice, tidal volume occurs most frequently during breathing that is neither conscious nor voluntary. It is an automatic movement that is constantly determined by the body's need for oxygen.

Increasing your air intake: inspiratory reserve volume (IRV)

You can boost the amplitude of each breath you take during inhalation. When you do this, the increase in volume of air beyond the tidal volume is called inspiratory reserve volume (IRV).

Depending on the size and physique of the person, this volume can vary between 2 and 3.5 liters of air.

You can breathe in different amounts of air. You can, for example, breathe in only a very slight amount of air, or, at the other extreme, as much as you possibly can (see pages 206 and 207).

IRV does not necessarily refer just to inhalation. For example, if you take in a deep breath and then exhale just enough to arrive at tidal volume, you are exhaling your IRV.

You may also stop breathing altogether (apnea) during inhalation or exhalation of IRV. This is referred to as "apnea of IRV."

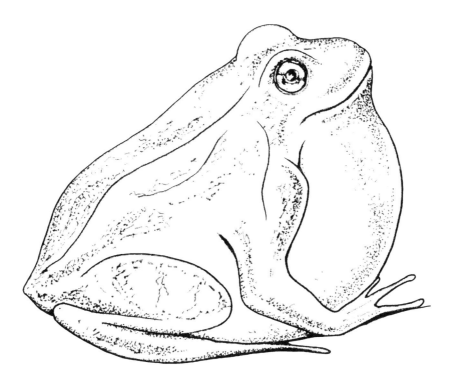

Increasing your air output:
expiratory reserve volume (ERV)

You can also empty the lungs more completely than during normal tidal breathing. This is often referred to as "forced exhalation."

When you exhale more air than in a normal relaxed exhalation, the difference in volume is referred to as expiratory reserve volume (ERV). This can vary between 1 and 1.2 liters of air depending on the individual (size, physique, training, medical disorders, etc.)

During ERV you can breathe out different amounts of air. You can, for example, exhale a very slight amount of air, or, at the other extreme, as much as you possibly can, for example, when you blow your nose or cough (see page 208).

ERV does not necessarily refer only to exhalation. For example, if you exhale deeply and then inhale just enough to arrive at tidal volume, you are inhaling your ERV.

You may also stop breathing altogether (apnea) during inhalation or exhalation of ERV. This is referred to as "apnea of ERV."

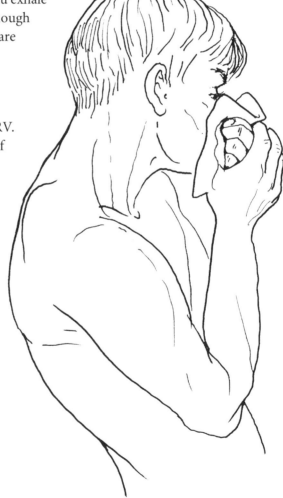

Residual volume (RV)

When you have exhaled the maximum amount of air, there will still be some air left in the lungs.

Even if you have exhaled as much air as you possibly can, e.g., coughing several times in a row without inhaling between coughs, there will still be a small amount of air left inside the lungs. This prevents the pulmonary alveoli from completely deflating and "sticking" together during exhalation, which would make it very difficult (if not impossible) to inhale again.

This air is referred to as residual volume (RV). It consists, on average, of 1–1.2 liters of air.

> All of the respiratory volumes described on the last few pages will vary considerably in amplitude depending on the size, physical fitness, and health of the individual.
>
> Here are a few examples:
>
> - By making the rib cage more flexible and limber, you can increase the amplitude of inhalation and thus of IRV.
>
> - By strengthening the muscles involved in exhalation, you can increase the amplitude of ERV.
>
> - A pathology affecting pulmonary elasticity (emphysema) may diminish the amplitude of ERV and boost the amplitude of RV (residual volume).

As you breathe, respiratory volumes can combine in different ways

For example, when you speak or sing, your breathing goes through the following stages:

1. You take a deep breath. This is a big IRV inhalation.

2. As you exhale, your breathing goes through the following stages:

    a. The volume passes through the IRV stage.

    b. The volume returns to tidal volume.

    c. As the volume falls below tidal volume, you go through ERV.

The practice pages include a few examples of how breathing strings together different respiratory volumes.

Two ways of representing respiratory volumes

One way is by looking at the change of volume in the alveoli of the lungs (the pulmonary alveoli are discussed on page 60).

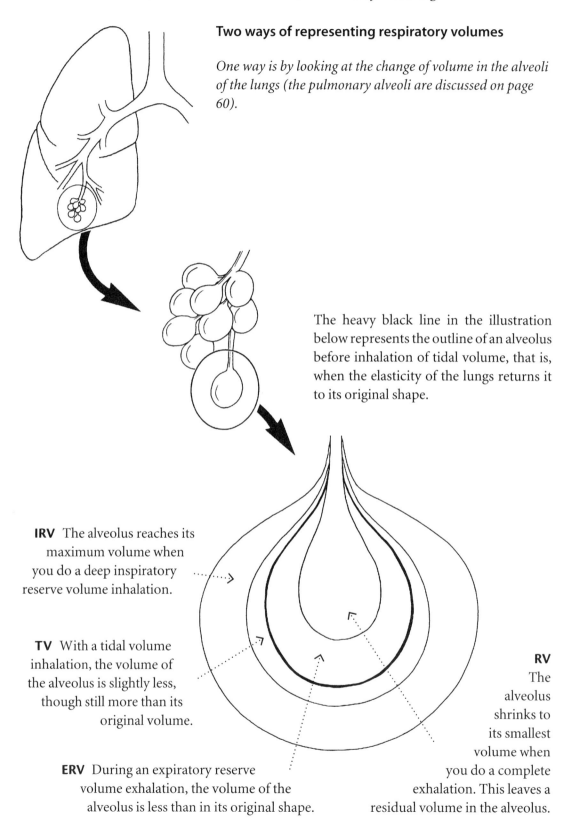

The heavy black line in the illustration below represents the outline of an alveolus before inhalation of tidal volume, that is, when the elasticity of the lungs returns it to its original shape.

IRV The alveolus reaches its maximum volume when you do a deep inspiratory reserve volume inhalation.

TV With a tidal volume inhalation, the volume of the alveolus is slightly less, though still more than its original volume.

RV The alveolus shrinks to its smallest volume when you do a complete exhalation. This leaves a residual volume in the alveolus.

ERV During an expiratory reserve volume exhalation, the volume of the alveolus is less than in its original shape.

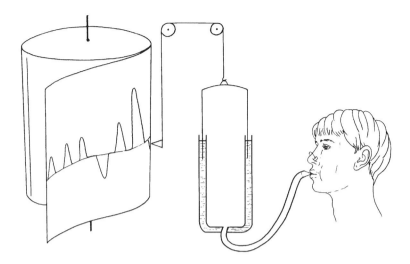

Another way is by measuring it on a spirometer (an instrument that measures breathing)

On a spirometer, the rising lines represent inhalations, while falling lines represent exhalations.

A horizontal line represents the volume when the lungs are at their most relaxed and elastic length.

At IRV the spirometer draws a line above the peak of the tidal volume at inhalation (upward line) and at exhalation (downward line).

The tidal volume appears as a smaller upward line at inhalation and a return to the horizontal line at exhalation.

At ERV the spirometer draws a line below the horizontal line, descending at exhalation and ascending at inhalation, that is, while returning from ERV.

This representation has some advantages: It helps you locate the inhalation and exhalation at each volume, which aids in determining all the forces involved in the process. It also makes it possible to "write" a movement with several successive breaths, sort of like a musical score.

However, there is an important problem with this representation: It makes it look as if inhalation is always an ascending movement. In fact, a lot of inhalations — though not all — involve a downward movement (of the diaphragm). So this representation can be a source of confusion with respect to how you envision the act of breathing.

RATES OF BREATHING

In normal breathing, respiration occurs at about 12 to 15 breaths of tidal volume per minute. This rate of airflow is therefore referred to as the *normal rate*.

You can modify the normal rate in the following ways:

- You can increase or decrease the frequency of breathing.

- You can change the rate of airflow during a single breath. For example, after a very slow inhalation, you can resume breathing at a normal rate.

- You can change the rate within a string of successive breaths. For example, you can inhale as fast as possible and then exhale as slowly as possible.

- You can also speed up or slow down the rate of airflow during a single breath. For example, you can inhale slowly at first, and then accelerate the inhalation, as if gaining momentum.

- The rate of breathing may also change for other reasons:
    - because of pathology
    - because you are adapting your breathing to a physical effort
    - because of emotions (often an involuntary change).

You can consciously change the rate of breathing, for example, when you train your breathing for speaking or singing (this is often done with voice training techniques).

However, variations in the rate of airflow still remain within the framework of the oxygen needs of the body.

The steepness of the slopes of the lines on the spirometer reflect the rate at which each breath occurs.

SECTION 1

· ·

Anatomical Pages

IN THE FOLLOWING pages (34-105) you will be introduced to the anatomical structures that are involved in breathing:

- bones and joints
- organs
- muscles associated with inhalation and exhalation.

These structures are involved with breathing in various ways based on their interactions with neighboring structures, forces, and respiratory volumes. These interactions are discussed on pages 107 through 157.

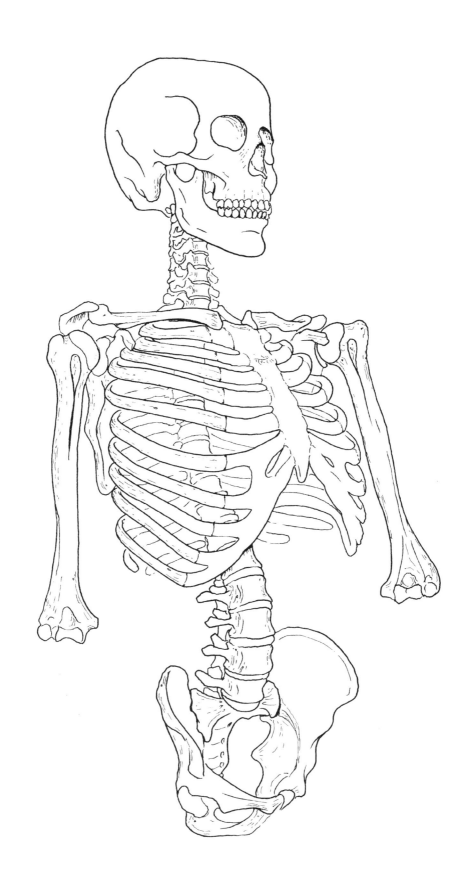

. . . .

CHAPTER TWO

The Skeleton's Role in Breathing

EVEN THOUGH BREATHING is an action that involves a gaseous mixture — air — the breathing apparatus itself is based on a bony framework. Because it is rigid, the skeleton provides a well-defined structure to breathing and stabilizes certain actions.

Many bones and cartilages are involved, and they in turn are linked by a number of joints which provide considerable mobility to the whole structure.

In this chapter, we will get to know the bones and articulations

- that are directly moved to make breathing possible, and

- that help support and act as a framework for the structures and muscles involved in breathing.

BONES SURROUNDING THE LUNGS

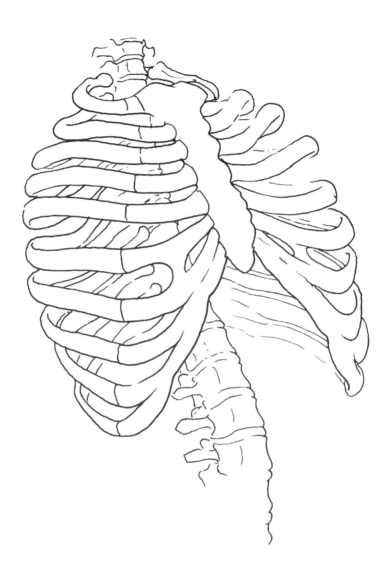

THORACIC "CAGE": A FLEXIBLE STRUCTURE

This is usually the first bony region people think of in the context of breathing, even though much of the act of breathing occurs without any movement in the thoracic cage.

It is sometimes confused with the thorax itself, which is a visceral area. The thoracic cage (or *rib cage*) possesses unique features which make it stand out among the bony structures of the skeleton:

- It consists of more than 80 joints. This arrangement makes it a very adaptable structure, similar to the foot, the hand, or even the spinal column.

- The malleability of the thoracic cage is enhanced by a property that is unique in the skeletal structure — the ribs are deformable and even elastic in their curvature:

  — *deformable* in that the individual ribs can be bent, more or less; they can withstand substantial torsion

  — *elastic* in that a rib which is forced out of its original shape will try to return to its shape in an elastic manner.

- The costal cartilages in the front, which connect the ribs to the sternum, constitute an area that is more flexible than the ribs themselves.

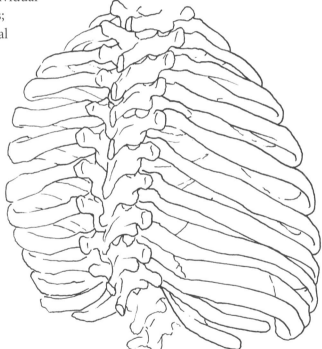

THORACIC CAGE AS A WHOLE

The thoracic cage consists of a number of elements:

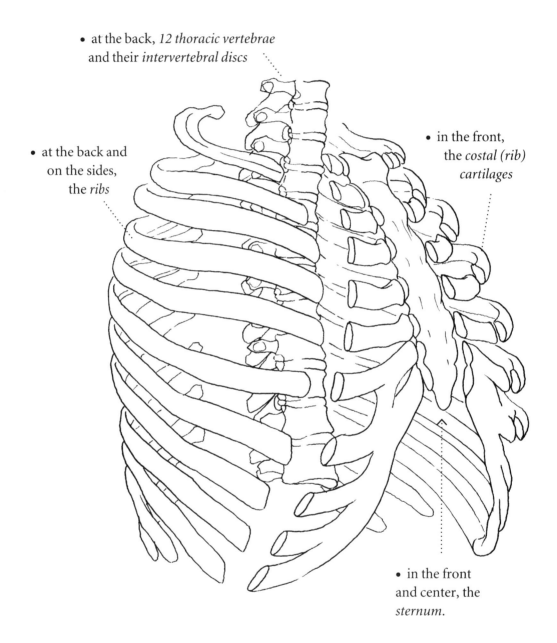

- at the back, *12 thoracic vertebrae* and their *intervertebral discs*

- at the back and on the sides, the *ribs*

- in the front, the *costal (rib) cartilages*

- in the front and center, the *sternum.*

These elements are not completely bony. Some of them belong to other functional structures. For example, the thoracic spine belongs to the spinal column, and the sternum is part of the shoulder girdle.

COSTAL ARC AND ITS ARTICULATIONS

Respiratory studies sometimes refer to the *costal arc*. This is not the same as a rib. The complete costal arc consists of:

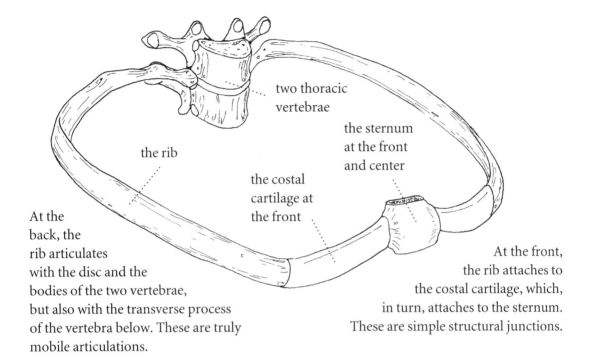

two thoracic
vertebrae

the sternum
at the front
and center

the rib

the costal
cartilage at
the front

At the
back, the
rib articulates
with the disc and the
bodies of the two vertebrae,
but also with the transverse process
of the vertebra below. These are truly
mobile articulations.

At the front,
the rib attaches to
the costal cartilage, which,
in turn, attaches to the sternum.
These are simple structural junctions.

The costal arc varies, depending on the rib level

The first one is especially small. At that level, the two arcs on the right and on the left outline the circle that the bottom of the neck forms with the top of the sternum.

The arcs of the 8TH through 10TH vertebrae are the largest and most flexible, considering the size of the rib and the costal cartilage.

The two last arcs are not complete because there is no costal cartilage at that level.

The costal arc is mobile

Its overall mobility is due to the mobility of each of its elements. It comprises the individual flexibility of each rib and the costal cartilage (see pages 41 and 42), but also the mobility of the costovertebral articulations (pages 47 and 48) and of the intervertebral articulations (pages 45 and 46). When working with the mobility of the costal arcs, all of these structures must be taken into account (see practice pages 162-165).

RIBS

The thoracic or rib cage consists of 12 pairs of ribs, which give it its shape.

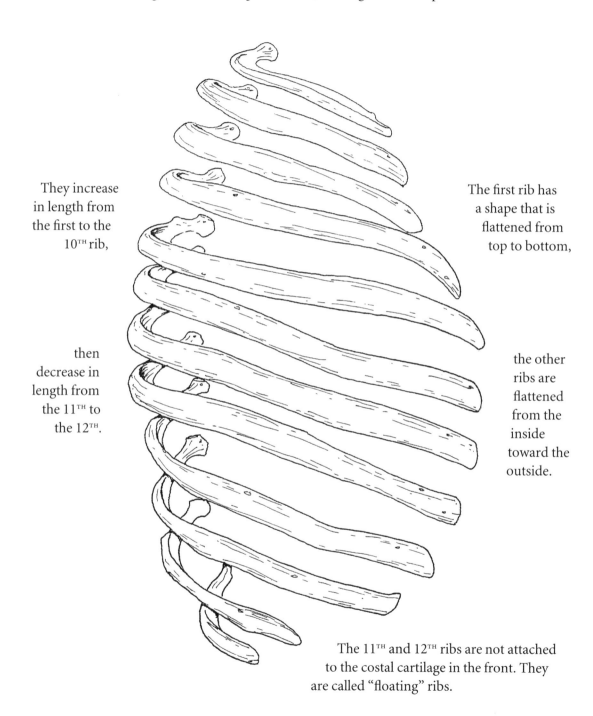

They increase in length from the first to the 10TH rib,

then decrease in length from the 11TH to the 12TH.

The first rib has a shape that is flattened from top to bottom,

the other ribs are flattened from the inside toward the outside.

The 11TH and 12TH ribs are not attached to the costal cartilage in the front. They are called "floating" ribs.

The individual rib

Each rib is a flat, flexible bone which consists of several parts:

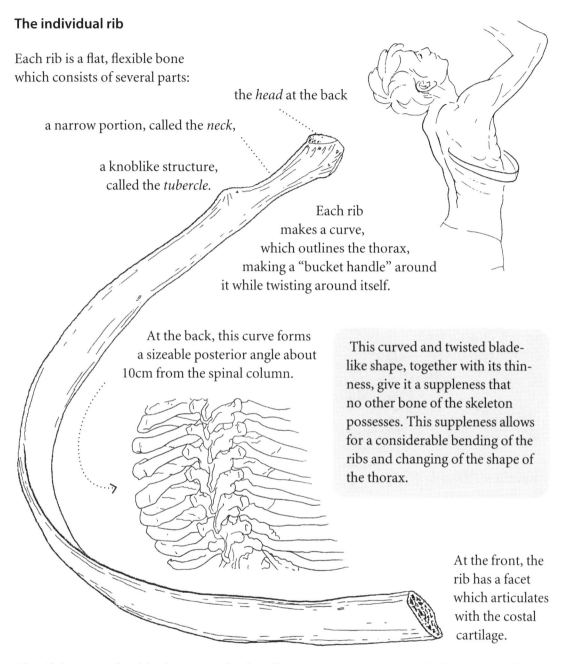

the *head* at the back

a narrow portion, called the *neck,*

a knoblike structure, called the *tubercle.*

Each rib makes a curve, which outlines the thorax, making a "bucket handle" around it while twisting around itself.

At the back, this curve forms a sizeable posterior angle about 10cm from the spinal column.

This curved and twisted blade-like shape, together with its thinness, give it a suppleness that no other bone of the skeleton possesses. This suppleness allows for a considerable bending of the ribs and changing of the shape of the thorax.

At the front, the rib has a facet which articulates with the costal cartilage.

The rib has considerable elasticity. After bending, it returns to its original shape. We will see that this elasticity sometimes contributes to the act of breathing, both during inhalation and exhalation.

The elasticity and suppleness of the ribs are maintained by movement, especially, but not exclusively, the movement of breathing. You can also actively or passively bend the ribs without breathing. (To maintain suppleness of the ribs, see practice pages 162-164.)

At the front, the ribs are attached to the sternum via the costal cartilage. The cartilage has the same curvature as the ribs. It consists of hyaline cartilage tissue, which is more supple and more elastic than bone tissue. That is why the area at the front of the thorax, to the left and right of the sternum, is more flexible, and permits greater amplitude in the act of breathing.

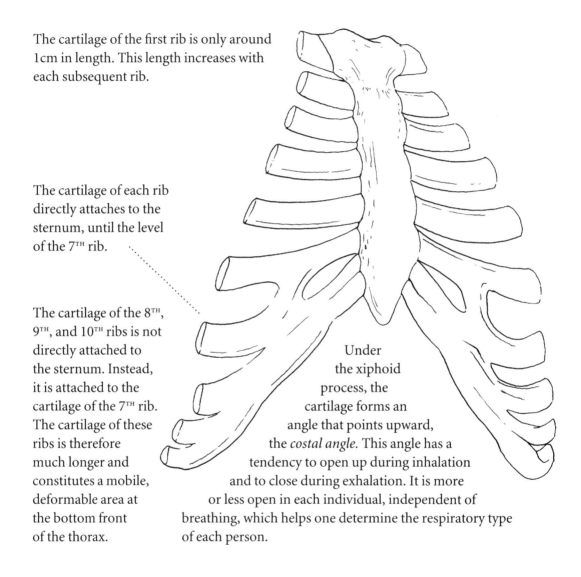

The cartilage of the first rib is only around 1cm in length. This length increases with each subsequent rib.

The cartilage of each rib directly attaches to the sternum, until the level of the 7TH rib.

The cartilage of the 8TH, 9TH, and 10TH ribs is not directly attached to the sternum. Instead, it is attached to the cartilage of the 7TH rib. The cartilage of these ribs is therefore much longer and constitutes a mobile, deformable area at the bottom front of the thorax.

Under the xiphoid process, the cartilage forms an angle that points upward, the *costal angle.* This angle has a tendency to open up during inhalation and to close during exhalation. It is more or less open in each individual, independent of breathing, which helps one determine the respiratory type of each person.

The suppleness of the costal cartilage adds to the suppleness of the ribs and the mobility of the costal and vertebral articulations. This is important to the amplitude and quality of breathing. The suppleness starts to decline as a person ages or if he or she lacks thoracic mobility. Conversely, it can be sustained by practicing breathing and non-breathing movements in the thoracic area (see practice pages 162-164).

STERNUM

The sternum is located at the upper, middle section of the rib cage. It is a flat bone, which is in a vertical position when a person is standing, and has the shape of a sword blade. It consists of three parts:

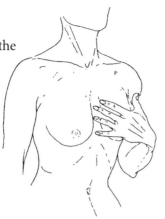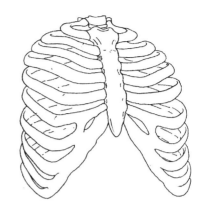

On its sides, the sternum has notches where the costal cartilage connects; this is called the costosternal junction.

- At the top is the *manubrium*, which articulates with the first two ribs.

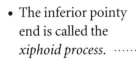

The first pair of notches are the clavicular notches, where the clavicles sit on the sternum.

The third pair of notches (for 2nd rib) are found at the junction of the manubrium with the body of the sternum. This junction is called the *angle of Louis*.

- The middle section, the longest, is the *body*, which articulates with ribs 3-7.

- The inferior pointy end is called the *xiphoid process*.

The 7TH notch, which is a bit larger than the others, connects with the costal cartilage of the 7TH rib, which then connects with the cartilage of ribs 8 through 10.

The sternum is an important landmark for observing and palpating respiratory movements. It can be moved vertically or obliquely to varying degrees, revealing how the diaphragm acts on the rib cage and how the inspiratory rib cage muscles work (see practice pages 190, 198, and 201).

SPINAL COLUMN DURING BREATHING

The spinal column serves as a skeletal link between the different regions of the body involved in breathing. Here we will consider the spinal column only in its relationship to breathing.

The spine serves as a *solid support structure*:

- for the neck and the head, where the inspiratory muscles attach: the sternocleidomastoid (SCM), the scalenes, and the serratus posterior superior

- for the rib cage, which is connected to the spine through about 40 articulations and numerous muscles; the rib cage can move around the spine or remain immobilized

- for the lumbar region, which contains the abdominal organs that are impacted by the diaphragm and the abdominal muscles

- for the sacrum, the back region of the pelvis where the muscles of the pelvic floor attach.

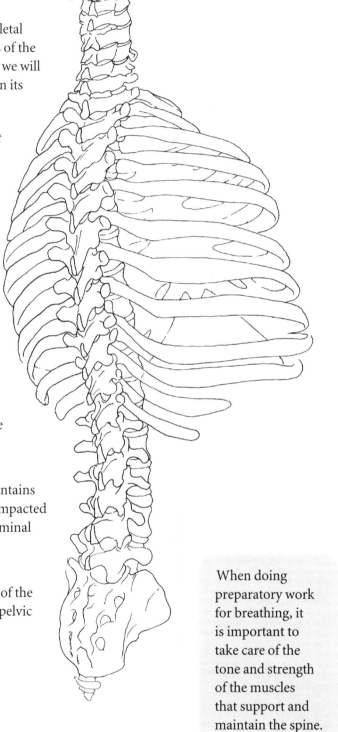

When doing preparatory work for breathing, it is important to take care of the tone and strength of the muscles that support and maintain the spine.

The spine is also like a *flexible flower stem*:
Its movements, especially at the thoracic level, influence
and/or complement the movements of the ribs.

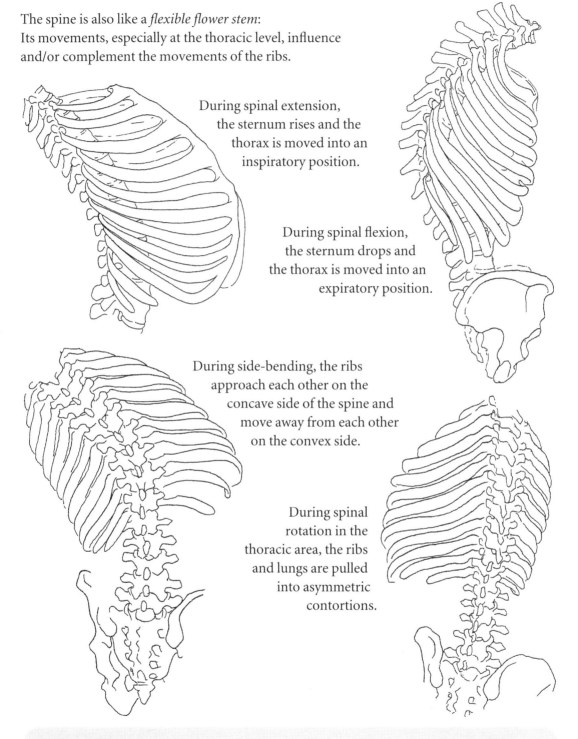

During spinal extension,
the sternum rises and the
thorax is moved into an
inspiratory position.

During spinal flexion,
the sternum drops and
the thorax is moved into an
expiratory position.

During side-bending, the ribs
approach each other on the
concave side of the spine and
move away from each other
on the convex side.

During spinal
rotation in the
thoracic area, the ribs
and lungs are pulled
into asymmetric
contortions.

When doing preparatory work for breathing, it is important to exercise the mobility
of the spinal column, especially at the thoracic level. Please refer to the preparatory
breathing exercises on pages 165-169.

Thoracic spine

This is the area of the spine that
corresponds to the rib cage.

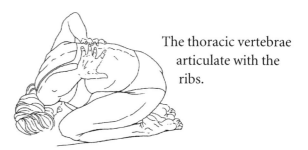

The thoracic vertebrae
articulate with the
ribs.

There are many articular surfaces, which
are covered with cartilage at the sides of
the vertebral bodies and at the front of the
transverse processes. All in all, this is the
least mobile part of the spinal column. Its
mobility is hindered by the presence of
the ribs, which are themselves attached to

the sternum. This is especially true for the
1ST through 7TH thoracic vertebrae. A little
lower, the ribs are attached to the sternum
through longer cartilage. Lower still, they
are not attached to the sternum at all. These
vertebrae are in fact the most mobile.

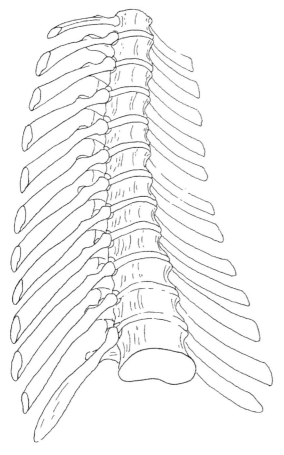

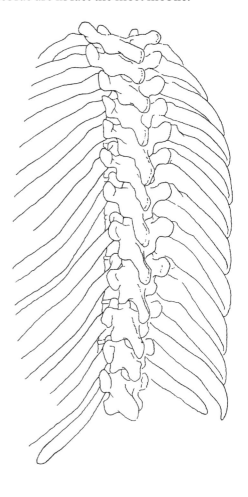

The ribs are attached to the thoracic spine by costovertebral articulations

At the back of the bodies of the thoracic vertebrae there are small articulating surfaces at the top and at the bottom. At every level, the surfaces of the two vertebrae stacked on top of one another, plus the intervertebral disc between them, form one single articulating area.

This area encloses the posterior portion of the rib (the head), which also has a small cartilaginous articulating surface.

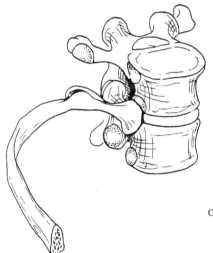

More to the back and on the outside, the tubercle of the rib articulates with the transverse process of the lower vertebra through small articular surfaces.

This second articulation joins the rib to a transverse process. Hence, *every rib attaches to the vertebrae via two articulations.* These articulations allow the ribs to pivot on their longitudinal axes and be raised and lowered.

Ligaments attach to these small articulations. Like every ligament, their main role is to hold the structures together, but they also have many sensory nerve endings. This is a favorite area for observing articular movements.

By moving these articulations, you will become increasingly aware of the breathing movements of the rib cage.

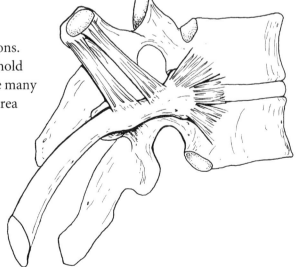

Variations in the axis of rib movement

The axis of movement is directed from inward to outward in the higher thoracic articulations (T1 through T5).

On this level, the ribs tend to move forward and upward. Thus, at the top of the thorax, the ribs move more to the front and back. The sternum therefore moves away from the spine and then back toward it, just like an old-fashioned pump.

In the lower articulations (T6 through T12), the axis is directed more from front to back. Thus, at this level, the ribs tend to move more toward the sides of the trunk, and each rib rises more like a bucket handle away from the sternum.

At the bottom of the thorax, the rib movement is easier and more extensive laterally.

These are just the tendencies of movement at each level; it does not mean that the ribs are limited to a specific direction there. Because of the flexibility of the ribs and the costal cartilage, all directions of movement are possible everywhere in the thoracic cage.

Some people prefer to breathe more in one way than another, which causes either a thorax that is more narrow and deep (when breathing more from front to back) or more flat and large (when breathing more laterally). To mobilize the ribs, it is important to exercise the ribs in both directions, especially when you are aware of a tendency to move them only in one direction.

A movement that elevates the ribs increases the diameter of the thorax

You can see that elevating the ribs laterally increases the frontal diameter of the thorax.

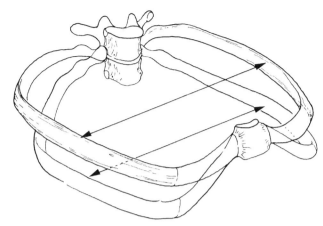

When you lift the ribs like a pump handle by changing their position from oblique to horizontal, you move the sternum away from the thoracic spine and enlarge the sagittal diameter of the thorax.

> *Note*: The same happens when the thoracic spine moves away from the sternum.
>
> This is the *main mechanism involved in thoracic breathing* (see page 141).
>
> It also explains why the *diaphragm pushes the ribs outward*, even though it is inside the thoracic cage (see page 138).

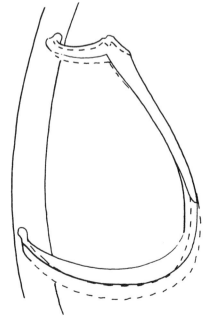

This is only true, however, when the ribs are in a low position. Beyond the horizontal plane, the elevation of the ribs does not really increase the diameter. In fact, beyond the horizontal plane, it can even lead to a reduction in the diameter.

Thus, an overly open position of the ribs at the beginning of an inhalation does not lead to an efficient thoracic inhalation, contrary to what is often thought (see page 135).

PELVIS

The pelvis is involved in breathing because it is at the bottom of the abdominal cavity. Here we will consider the pelvis only in its relationship to breathing.

The pelvis is a bony structure at the base of the trunk, which looks both like a container for the organs and also like a solid ring which connects the trunk with the lower limbs.

It consists of four bones: the two *hip bones*, the *sacrum*, and the *coccyx*.

Here are some landmarks:

1. the *iliac crest*, where you "put your hands on your hips"

2. its most anterior portion, the *anterior superior iliac spine*

3. the *pubic symphysis*, or joint between the two pubic bones

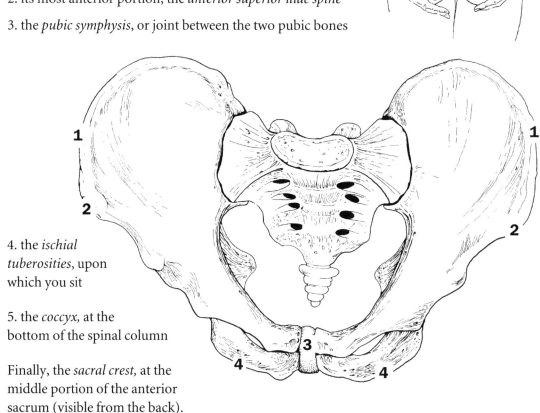

4. the *ischial tuberosities*, upon which you sit

5. the *coccyx*, at the bottom of the spinal column

Finally, the *sacral crest*, at the middle portion of the anterior sacrum (visible from the back).

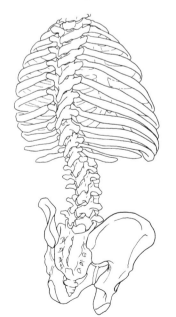

The pelvis consists of two parts:

- The *greater pelvis* is large and open in the front. It contains the lower abdominal organs and the abdominal muscles insert into it.

- The *lesser pelvis*, which is completed at the bottom by the muscles of the pelvic floor, contains the pelvic organs.

The pelvis connects to the femurs via the *hip joints*, which enable you to rotate the thighs in different directions. The most well-known movement you can perform is the rocking movement, in which you tilt the pelvis forward (anteversion) and backward (retroversion).

The *lumbar vertebrae* extend from the pelvis upward and form the posterior wall of the abdominal cavity. They connect the pelvis to the thoracic cage.

The five lumbar vertebrae are massive, and many respiratory muscles attach to them: the diaphragm, transversus abdominis, quadratus lumborum, and serratus posterior inferior.

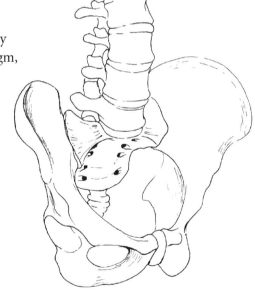

Because the pelvis and thoracic cage are linked together through the lumbar vertebrae, they behave interdependently.

The movement of either one will influence the contents—the organs—of the other, shaping them and also influencing the breathing (see pages 115, 127, 128, and 147).

SHOULDER GIRDLE

The shoulder girdle consists of bones and joints that attach the trunk to the upper limbs. Here we will consider the shoulder girdle only in its relationship to breathing.

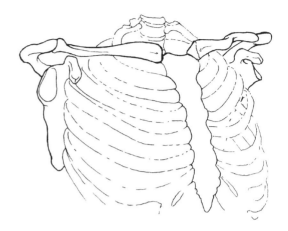

This structure is involved in breathing:

- via many inspiratory costal muscles which attach to it

- via its position and movements, which influence the thorax and move it into a greater or lesser inspiratory or expiratory position.

This girdle consists of the *sternum*, the two *clavicles*, and the two *scapulae*.

The *clavicle,* or collar bone, is a small bone which rests at the front of the thorax between the sternum and the scapula. Viewed from the front, it looks almost straight; viewed from below, it has an S-shape, which partially follows the outline of the top of the ribs.

The *scapula,* or shoulder blade, is a flat, triangular bone, which rests on the posterior and lateral portions of the top ribs. Its internal surface flattens against the thorax and glides upon it; its external surface is below the skin and is covered by many muscles.

Articulations of the shoulder girdle

Its bones are joined to each other by articulations that are relatively free and small:

- The *sternoclavicular joint* links the sternum to the clavicle. Its cartilaginous surface has the shape of an inverse interlocking saddle, which allows the clavicle to move in different directions from the sternum. For example, it enables lifting and lowering of the shoulders, and moving them forward and backward.

- The *acromioclavicular joint* is located between the clavicle and the scapula. Its surface is small, oval, and flat. This joint is less mobile than the sterno-clavicular joint, but it helps the scapula to complete the movements of the clavicle.

In addition to being mobile, these articulations add to the movements that the shoulders can perform, and thus to the movements of the arm.

In practice, the movements of the shoulder and of the rib cage often blend. We frequently inhale while raising our shoulders.

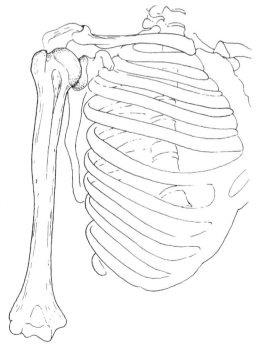

Humerus

This is the bone of the upper arm. It is involved in breathing because the pectoralis major, one of the main inspiratory muscles, attaches here.

The humerus meets with the scapula at the *scapulohumeral joint*, where the ball-shaped head of the humerus fits into the socket-shaped glenoid cavity of the scapula.

Cervical vertebrae

These vertebrae comprise the top part of the spinal column. They are smaller than the other vertebrae. The first two, the *atlas* (C1) and the *axis* (C2), differ considerably from the others. The remaining five vertebrae have the typical shape of the other vertebrae.

The cervical vertebrae are involved in breathing for two primary reasons:

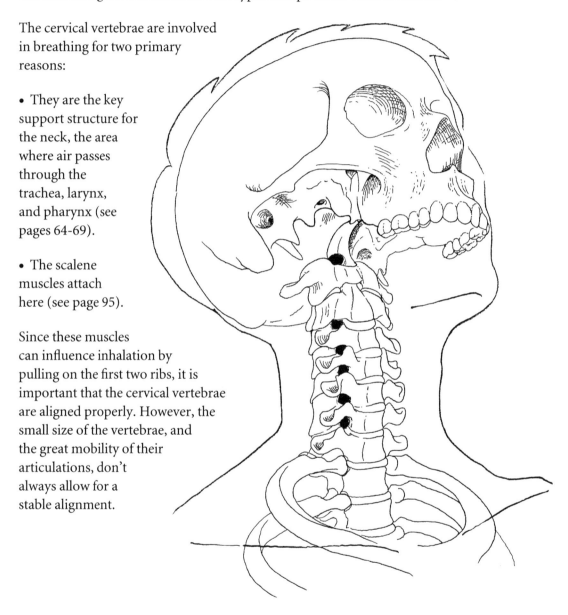

• They are the key support structure for the neck, the area where air passes through the trachea, larynx, and pharynx (see pages 64-69).

• The scalene muscles attach here (see page 95).

Since these muscles can influence inhalation by pulling on the first two ribs, it is important that the cervical vertebrae are aligned properly. However, the small size of the vertebrae, and the great mobility of their articulations, don't always allow for a stable alignment.

In particular, the last cervical vertebra (C7) articulates with the first thoracic vertebra, which attaches to the first rib. This is the *cervicothoracic junction*, where the cervical hypermobility abruptly changes to the upper thoracic hypomobility. Frequently, this base of the cervical spine is in flexion all the time and loses its mobility.

CRANIAL BONES

These bones are part of the structures involved in breathing. Some of the muscles of respiration also insert here.

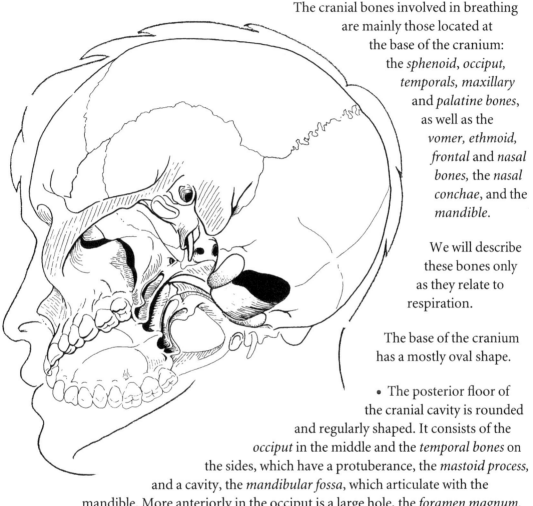

The cranial bones involved in breathing are mainly those located at the base of the cranium: the *sphenoid, occiput, temporals, maxillary* and *palatine bones,* as well as the *vomer, ethmoid, frontal* and *nasal bones,* the *nasal conchae,* and the *mandible.*

We will describe these bones only as they relate to respiration.

The base of the cranium has a mostly oval shape.

• The posterior floor of the cranial cavity is rounded and regularly shaped. It consists of the *occiput* in the middle and the *temporal bones* on the sides, which have a protuberance, the *mastoid process,* and a cavity, the *mandibular fossa,* which articulate with the mandible. More anteriorly in the occiput is a large hole, the *foramen magnum.* At its anterior margin, the occiput narrows slightly and articulates with the *sphenoid bone.*

• The anterior half of the cranial base is much more complicated:

Here, we can find the *hard palate,* which is bordered by the superior dental arcades. It consists of the two *maxillary bones* at the front and the *palatine bones* at the back. This area clearly projects more inferiorly than the remainder of the cranial base.

Higher up in this area are the bones that form the *nasal skeleton* (see pages 72 and 73).

The *mandible* will be discussed in the context of the mouth (see pages 74 and 75).

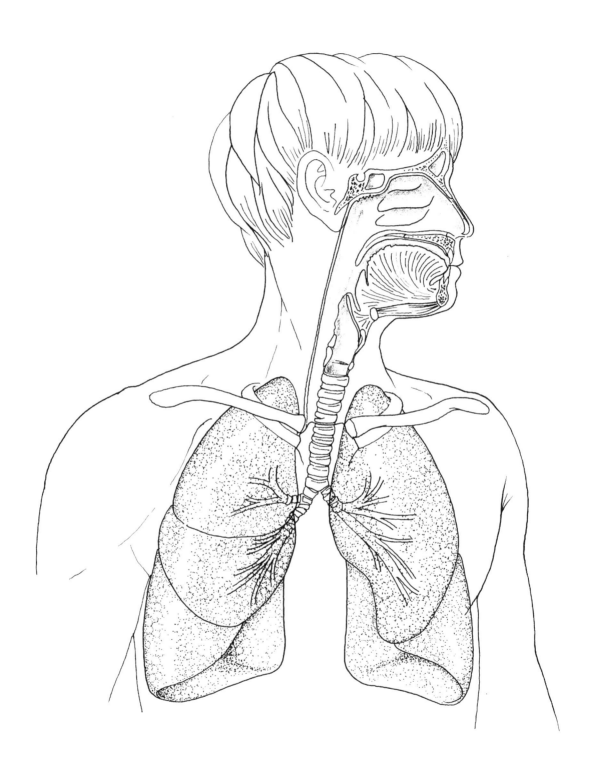

. . . .

CHAPTER THREE

Respiratory Organs

THERE ARE SOME who insist that breathing is an activity that involves the entire body. That is true in the sense that respiratory movement extends into the extremities. It is also true in the sense that breathing has a considerable influence on all the physiological functions of the body, far beyond what is referred to as the respiratory system. And finally, it is true in the sense that the act of breathing mobilizes both the thorax and the abdomen.

However, the respiratory organs, strictly speaking, are only located in three different areas: the *thorax, neck,* and *head.*

The *thorax* mainly houses the lungs, the functional organs of respiration, that is, they are responsible for the active function of breathing or ventilation.

The *neck* and *head* contain the structural conduits of the respiratory system, which have a more passive role in respiration: these are the *airway passages.* They can be divided into *superior airway passages* in the head and neck, and *inferior airway passages* in the thorax.

These passages may nevertheless actively influence breathing by restricting the airflow on different levels and with different force.

LUNGS: WHERE BLOOD AND AIR MEET

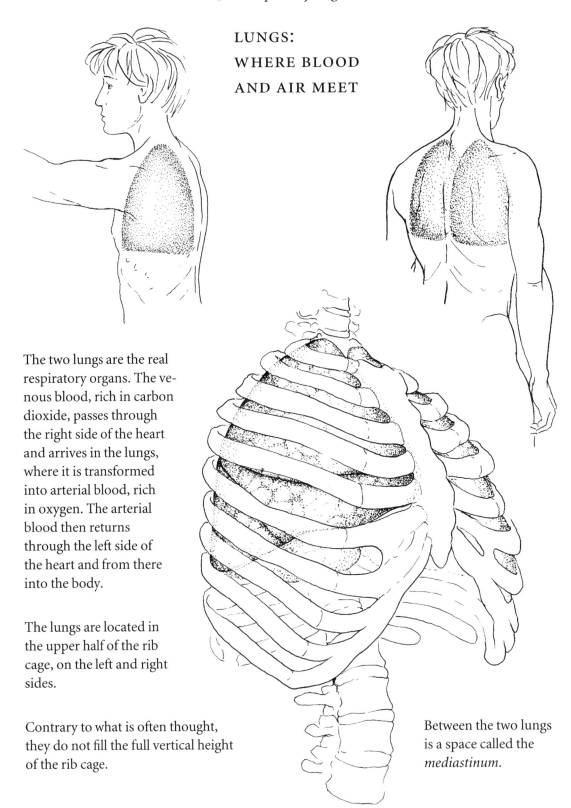

The two lungs are the real respiratory organs. The venous blood, rich in carbon dioxide, passes through the right side of the heart and arrives in the lungs, where it is transformed into arterial blood, rich in oxygen. The arterial blood then returns through the left side of the heart and from there into the body.

The lungs are located in the upper half of the rib cage, on the left and right sides.

Contrary to what is often thought, they do not fill the full vertical height of the rib cage.

Between the two lungs is a space called the *mediastinum.*

Each of the two lungs is shaped like a rounded cone.

The slightly rounded superior portion of the lungs is
called the *apex*. It occupies the
upper part of the rib cage and
even juts up a little above the
first rib.

The hollow portion
of the lungs that is
turned toward the
mediastinum is
called the *hilum*.

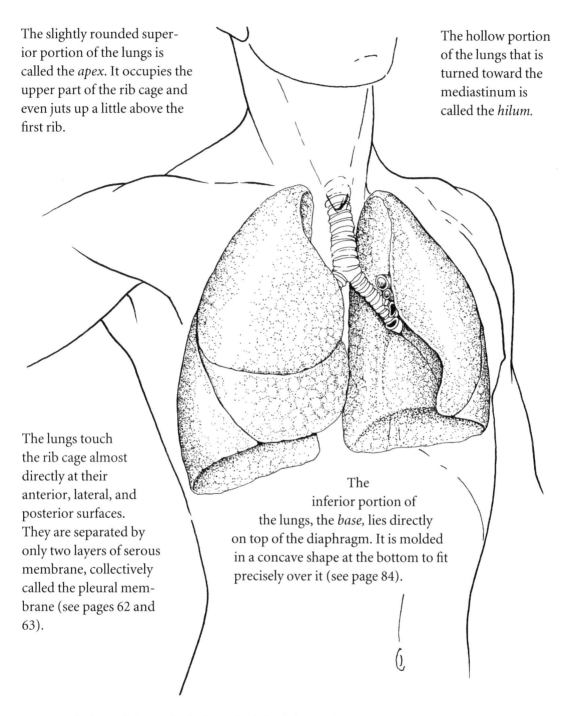

The lungs touch
the rib cage almost
directly at their
anterior, lateral, and
posterior surfaces.
They are separated by
only two layers of serous
membrane, collectively
called the pleural mem-
brane (see pages 62 and
63).

The
inferior portion of
the lungs, the *base,* lies directly
on top of the diaphragm. It is molded
in a concave shape at the bottom to fit
precisely over it (see page 84).

Because the heart is located a little to the left of the median line, the two lungs do not have the
same size or shape: The right lung is bigger than the left. The medial surfaces of both lungs are
hollow, and the left lung fits into the shape of the heart.

PULMONARY ALVEOLI

Each lung has many little sacs containing *pulmonary alveoli*, out of which emerge very fine *alveolar ducts* (see page 64).

There is a significant number of alveoli, about 300 million. If you were to unfold their cellular walls, it would cover an area of 150 square meters. They are grouped into *pulmonary lobules*.

This is where the exchange of oxygen and carbon dioxide occurs, between the air coming in from the outside and the blood circulating in the capillaries.

The walls of the alveoli have a very thin lining made of *epithelial tissue*,* crisscrossed by a network of *capillary vessels* that are as fine as hairs. This layer is the *alveolar-capillary membrane*, through which the respiratory gases from the blood and air diffuse.

*Two of the four basic types of tissue found in the body are the *epithelial tissue*, which lines other structures, and the *connective tissue*, which supports and gives structure to the body.

The lungs are like a rubber band

Another aspect of the lungs, which is little known, is that the alveoli contain connective tissue that is exceptionally rich in *elastic fibers*.

To the right, you see a cut through a pulmonary lobule, which shows the epithelial tissue covering the inside of the alveoli. (The cells are shaped like little cobblestones.) Between the alveoli are layers of connective tissue, which are crisscrossed by vessels, among other structures. The connective tissue also contains collagen fibers and many elastic fibers.

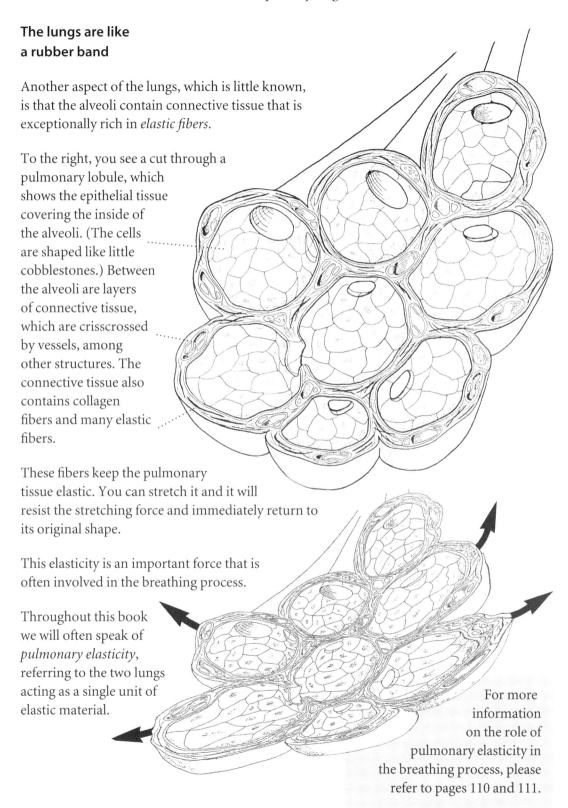

These fibers keep the pulmonary tissue elastic. You can stretch it and it will resist the stretching force and immediately return to its original shape.

This elasticity is an important force that is often involved in the breathing process.

Throughout this book we will often speak of *pulmonary elasticity*, referring to the two lungs acting as a single unit of elastic material.

For more information on the role of pulmonary elasticity in the breathing process, please refer to pages 110 and 111.

PLEURAL MEMBRANE: DOUBLE ENVELOPE OF THE LUNGS

The *pleurae* are membranes which wrap around a large portion of the lungs. Each lung has a pleura, one for the right and one for the left. In addition, each of the pleurae has two layers.

In fact, each pleura is shaped like an individual pocket that is doubled over, kind of like a deflated rubber ball, which is folded inward so that it can wrap around the lungs.

Thus, each pleura wraps around the lungs in a double layer. It leaves an open area at the pulmonary pedicle, the area where the pleura folds on itself.

The inner layer of the pleura is called the *visceral pleura.* It takes on the shape of the lungs, to which it adheres.

The outer layer is called the *parietal pleura.* It attaches to the deep surface of the ribs and the superior surface of the diaphragm, whose movement it follows. It is slightly bigger than the lungs, which allows it to change volume during breathing.

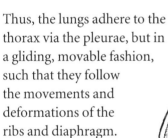

Between these two layers is a partially open space. (This space changes continuously depending on the atmospheric and intrapulmonary pressures.)

These two layers are sucked toward and adhere to one another. Hence, the lungs stay glued to the ribs and the diaphragm.

Between the two layers there is a small amount of *pleural fluid,* which is secreted by certain pleural cells. This fluid allows the two layers to glide on one another.

Thus, the lungs adhere to the thorax via the pleurae, but in a gliding, movable fashion, such that they follow the movements and deformations of the ribs and diaphragm.

(The opposite is true as well. The lungs, through their elastic force, cause the ribs and the diaphragm to move and deform with them.)

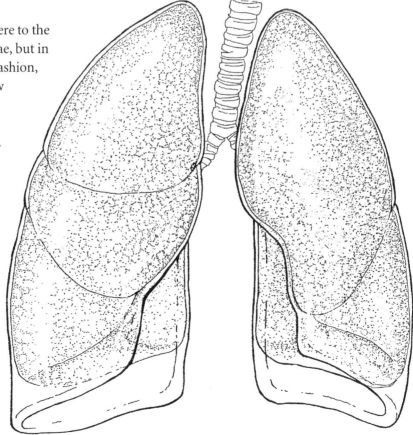

AIRWAY PASSAGES

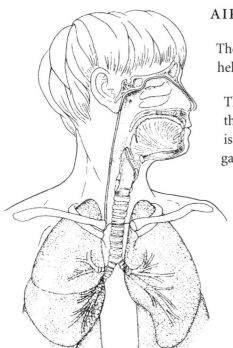

These passages include all the areas and conduits that help move the air to and from the lungs.

This part of the respiratory system is sometimes called the "anatomic dead space." Why? Because the air that is found here does not participate in the exchange of gasses.

Inferior airway passages

Part of these structures are found in or just outside of the lungs: the *bronchi*. These are airways that are shaped like a pipe.

"Bronchial tree"

The two big *primary bronchi*, which run from the trachea to the lungs, divide into *secondary (lobar) bronchi*, one for each lobe of the lungs.

Each bronchus divides again several times inside its lobe, forming *tertiary (segmental) bronchi*, which in turn divide into *bronchioles*. These divide even further into smaller and smaller bronchioles, until they branch into *alveolar ducts*, which are extremely small.

The primary and secondary bronchi are wrapped in circular cartilage, which keeps them open. Then, in the tertiary bronchi, there are still plates of cartilage, but they do not form a complete ring around the bronchi. The bronchioles do not have any cartilage, nor do the alveolar ducts.

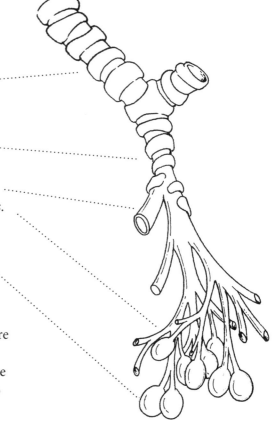

The entire structure forms the shape of a tree without leaves.

The deep inferior airways are lined with a *moist mucous membrane*, which has one peculiarity. It is lined with miniscule *cilia*, which move during breathing.

The cilia have a very important role. Through their movement they bring the mucus, which is formed in the alveoli and the smaller bronchi, up toward the exit of the respiratory system. This mucus, which is necessary for the function and maintenance of the alveoli, must be constantly evacuated through the pharynx, where it can be swallowed and digested. Deterioration of these cilia (especially in smokers) causes an obstruction of the lungs, preventing them from properly evacuating the mucus. The result is an infection, called bronchitis.

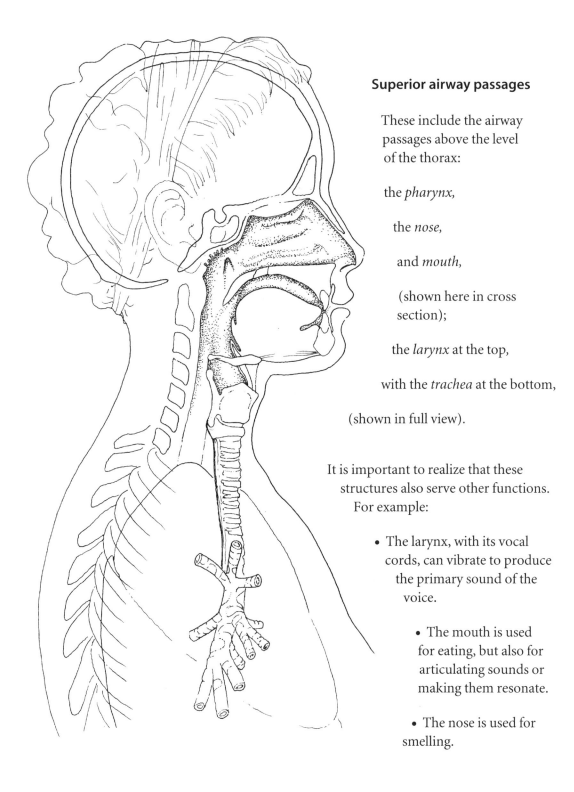

Superior airway passages

These include the airway passages above the level of the thorax:

the *pharynx,*

the *nose,*

and *mouth,*

(shown here in cross section);

the *larynx* at the top,

with the *trachea* at the bottom,

(shown in full view).

It is important to realize that these structures also serve other functions. For example:

- The larynx, with its vocal cords, can vibrate to produce the primary sound of the voice.

  - The mouth is used for eating, but also for articulating sounds or making them resonate.

  - The nose is used for smelling.

Trachea

Situated in the lower half of the neck and partly superior to the thorax, the trachea is an airway passage that extends from the larynx at the top to the primary bronchi at the bottom.

It is a pipe-shaped structure with a length of about 10cm (4 inches), which can vary depending on the position of the neck and the breathing process.

This pipe stays open due to a framework of cartilaginous rings, which are almost circular. Its posterior part has a supple, elastic membrane. Its deep surface is lined with a mucosa.

This arrangement makes it a semi-rigid passageway: The trachea is always open for the passage of air.

To allow for swallowing of bigger pieces of food, it can also adapt to deformations in the esophagus, which sits right behind it.

It is also flexible enough to adapt to various movements of the head and neck, and of breathing.

Larynx: where breathing occurs and the voice is born

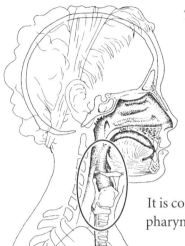

The larynx, which sits on top of the trachea, is a very large, complicated, and specialized structure.

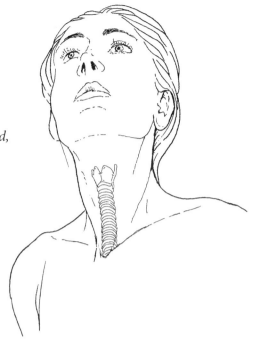

It is connected with the pharynx at the top.

It consists of a "skeleton" made from several cartilages.

At the top of the trachea, the *cricoid cartilage* resembles a thickened ring.

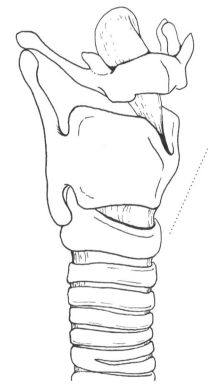

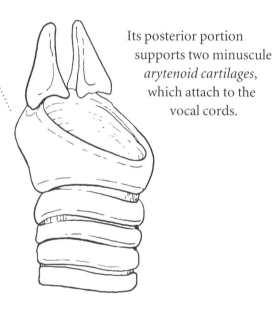

Its posterior portion supports two minuscule *arytenoid cartilages*, which attach to the vocal cords.

Partial front view of the larynx

Partial front view of the cricoid cartilage

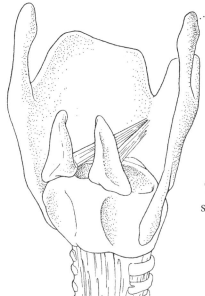

Partial back view
of the larynx

Just above is the *thyroid cartilage,* the largest of the cartilages (not to be confused with the gland of the same name), which is shaped like a book that opens to the back. Vocal cords are also attached to this structure.

Its contour is very prominent at the middle of the neck: This is the "Adam's apple," which is larger in males than in females.

The inside of the entire structure is covered with a mucosa, so that instead of two cords, only two *folds* are visible.

The vocal cords can be brought together or moved apart and/or stretched, depending on the position of the cartilages to which they attach. The position of the cartilages changes the space between the vocal cords. This variable space is called the *glottis.*

Overhanging the glottis is another cartilage shaped like the tongue of a shoe, the *epiglottis* (1). It can shut down and obstruct the air passage. In practice, the epiglottis closes during eating (2). This prevents food or drink from entering the trachea.

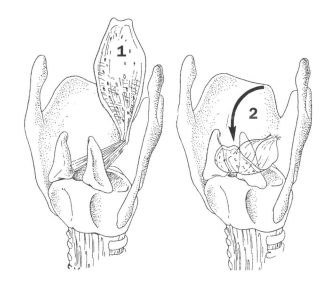

The larynx is like a sphincter, which allows more or less air to pass through.

When the vocal cords are completely closed, there is no glottal space. This position can prevent the passage of air. You can feel this, for example, during a hiccup or just before a coughing attack. The slow down in the passage of air can be more or less complete (see page 130).

The larynx is also where the first sound of the voice is made.

The air arrives at the glottis where it comes in contact with the vocal cords, causing them to vibrate. This produces the "source sound" of the human voice, which is then filtered and further developed in the resonance chambers situated below.

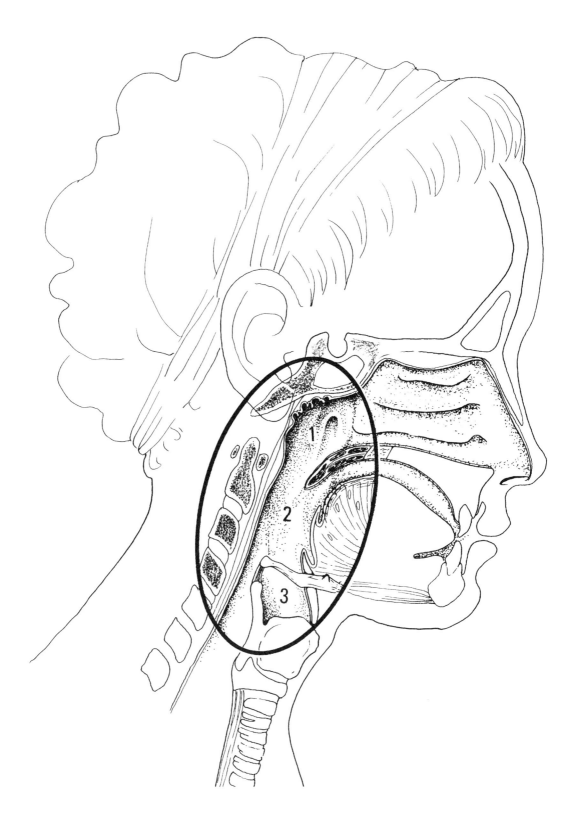

Pharynx (or throat)

The *pharynx*, or throat, is about 12cm in length and connects the posterior parts of the nose and mouth to the top of the larynx and esophagus.

The back of the pharynx is a continuous tube with a fibrous wall composed of muscles and lined with mucous membrane. It runs from the base of the cranium down the anterior surface of the cervical spine.

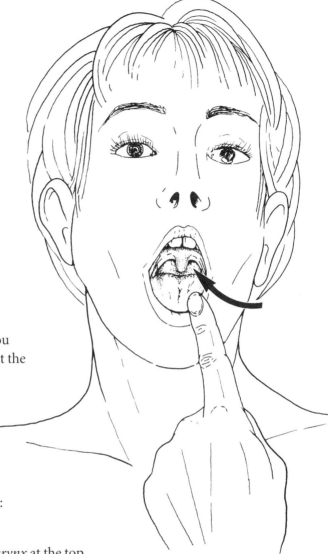

When the mouth is opened wide, you can see the mucosa of the pharynx at the bottom of the throat.

As shown on the opposite page, the anterior portion of the pharynx consists of the following parts, from top to bottom:

1. posterior to the nose: the *nasopharynx* at the top

2. posterior to the mouth: the *oropharynx* at mid-level

3. posterior to the hyoid bone: the *laryngopharynx* at the bottom.

Air inhaled through the nose passes through all three levels; air inhaled through the mouth only passes through the bottom two levels.

Nose

The nose, which is the most visible part of the respiratory system, is one of two passageways for air to pass between the outside and inside of the body.

(It is also possible to breathe through the mouth, as we shall see later.)

On the outside, the nose has a midline ridge that is more or less prominent.

At the bottom, on each side of the ridge, are the *alae nasi*, or wings of the nose, which skirt the *nostrils*.

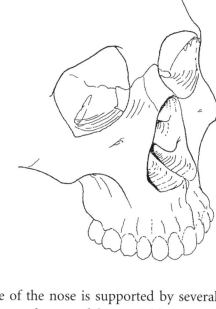

The external shape of the nose is supported by several juxtaposed *cartilages* and some of the cranial bones: the *maxillae, vomer,* and the *nasal and frontal bones.*

This entire part of the nose forms the *vestibule of the anterior portion of the nose.*

Behind the vestibule, the nose forms two openings that are separated from each other by the nasal septum: the *nasal cavities.*

These cavities extend:

- at the top, to the area where the olfactory nerve endings emerge (the region of the ethmoid and frontal bones)

- in the back, to orifices, called *internal nares (choanae),* which start in the highest region of the pharynx, the *nasopharynx.*

Inside the nasal cavities, the skeleton of the nasal structure is completed in the lateral walls by minuscule bones, called *nasal conchae,* which ensure that the internal space of the nasal cavities contains many recesses and creases, instead of being smooth. The entire internal structure is lined with moist, warm mucosa.

The air circulating in this area does not flow in a direct line, but is moved around through small ridges called *turbinates,* which warm up and humidify the air.

Numerous hairs line the internal mucous membrane. They are responsible for filtering out dust particles and thus purify the air before it enters the lungs. The mucosae contain cells that secrete a *sticky mucus,* which contains an *antibacterial enzyme.*

Mouth

The mouth is not the preferred passageway for air during breathing. In contrast to the nose, it does not have the means to purify and humidify the air.

Nevertheless, there are many occasions where you might breathe through the mouth, for example, when you want to breathe faster or heavier, when you swim, or when you sing.

That is why it is appropriate to describe the mouth here as a possible passageway for air, as well as a possible hindrance to the passage of air.

The anterior portion of the mouth is lined with the *lips*.

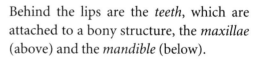

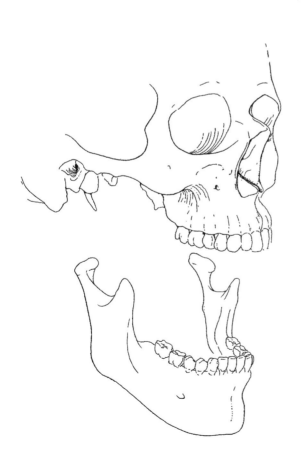

Behind the lips are the *teeth*, which are attached to a bony structure, the *maxillae* (above) and the *mandible* (below).

The mandible articulates with the cranium via the *temporomandibular joint (TMJ)*. The mandible is covered by mucosae, which make up the *gingiva (gums)*.

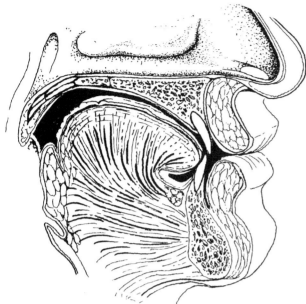

Surrounded by the teeth, the *tongue* is located in the bottom of the mouth. Even though the visible portion (the tip of the tongue) is small, it forms a sizeable mass toward the back, which extends all the way to the floor of the mouth and, behind it, to the pharynx. The tongue has 17 muscles and can therefore perform a number of different actions.

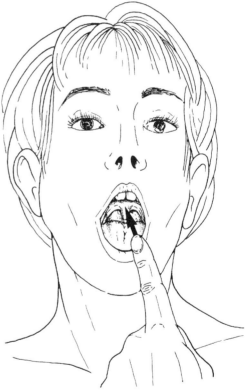

At the top, the mouth is bordered by the *palate,* which is divided into two parts:

• The anterior part, or *hard palate,* is formed by the *maxillae* and the *palatine bones.*

• The posterior part (the posterior third of the palate), or *soft palate,* extends the palate to the back. It is a layer, formed by ten muscles, which can go up, or down, stretch, and perform many different actions during speaking or yawning, for example. It is the soft palate which vibrates during snoring.

At the back, the mouth is bordered by palatoglossal muscles, forming a narrowing structure called the *palatoglossal arch* (which is where the palatine *tonsils* are located).

The entire palatal structure (hard and soft palate) and the palatoglossal muscles are covered by mucosae.

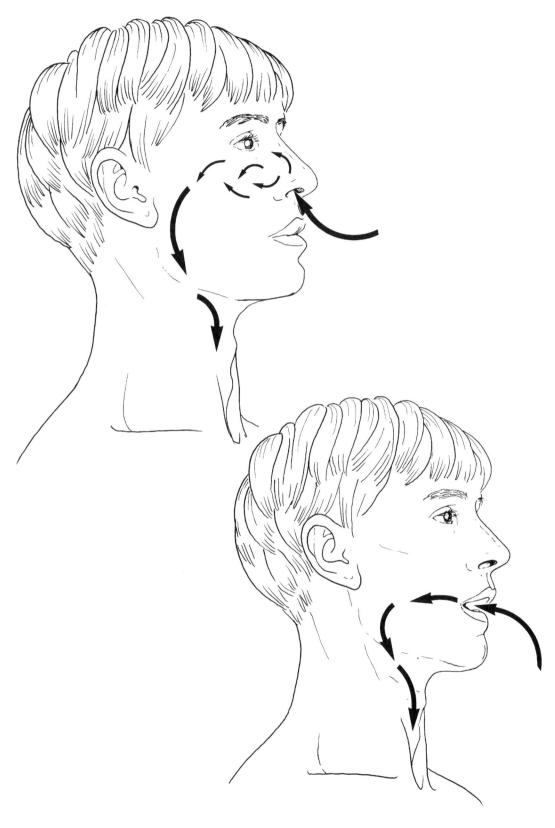

Breathing through the nose or the mouth?

In many physical activities, instructors often teach their students to breathe a certain way in a rather dogmatic fashion.

In fact, both ways of breathing — through the nose and through the mouth — are possible, and each has its advantages and disadvantages.

When you breathe through the nose

As we have seen on page 73, the air is:

- warmed up and humidified by the mucosae
- cleaned of dust particles, which the hairs or the mucus filter out
- cleaned of bacteria through enzymes in the mucus.

Thus, the air that reaches the lungs is warm, purified, and of good quality. From this point of view, it is better to breathe through the nose.*

In addition, the nerve endings of the olfactory nerve, located at the top of the nose, are stimulated more during nasal breathing. This is especially true if you only breathe in through one nostril because more air enters the nasal cavity.

When you breathe through the mouth

- When the mouth is open, the air does not meet as much resistance since the passageway is larger (the back of the mouth is larger than the back of the nose, which is often very narrow). The passageway is also slightly shorter. Thus, you can more easily inhale or exhale larger quantities of air through an open mouth.

It's easier to do deeper breathing through the mouth, circulating larger volumes of air. This is especially helpful when you want to quickly breathe a lot of air:

- during intense physical activity
- when trying to inhale air quickly (e.g., swimming, singing, or playing wind instruments)
- for techniques requiring the deepest exhalation possible (e.g., when stretching the diaphragm).

- When inhaling or exhaling through the mouth, you can also *vary the airflow* more easily than when you breathe through the nose. You can close the mouth more or less, especially at the level of the lips, tongue, and soft palate (see page 130 on the occlusives).

....

* Sometimes it is difficult or even impossible to breathe through the nose. This is often due to either malpositioning of the tongue or narrow air passages in the nasopharynx.

CHAPTER FOUR

. . . .

Respiratory Muscles

MANY DIFFERENT MUSCLES can influence the action of breathing. For most of them, this is not their main function.

Some are inspiratory muscles. They expand the lungs.

Some are expiratory muscles. They "close" the lungs.

Some muscles influence both inhalation and exhalation, depending on how their action combines with the actions of other muscles.

But all of these muscles often have an *indirect influence* on respiration. For example, they may slow down or completely stop breathing. Or they may make breathing possible by relaxing.

Finally, it is important to remember that there are certain aspects of breathing that occur *without muscular action*. (Please refer to the discussion of respiratory volumes and the forces that influence those volumes.)

MUSCLES OF INSPIRATION

These are the muscles that help *increase the volume of the lungs*. Expansion of the lungs can occur in two different ways:

- by applying a pulling action to the base of the lungs

- by applying a pulling action at the anterior, lateral, or posterior surfaces of the lungs.

The first inspiratory muscle that we will look at here is the diaphragm. It can act in both ways.

Diaphragm: primary inspiratory muscle

Most regular breathing occurs because of this muscle. It acts like a pump at the base of the lungs.

The diaphragm is a large muscular and fibrous wall which simultaneously separates and connects the thorax and the abdomen.

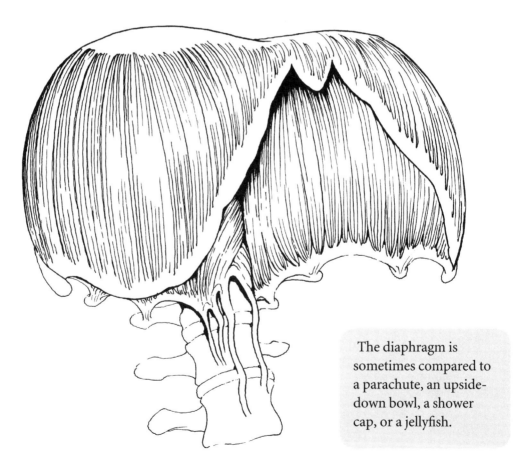

The diaphragm is sometimes compared to a parachute, an upside-down bowl, a shower cap, or a jellyfish.

The diaphragm is situated between the organs like a supple layer which fits between them and takes their form. It is shaped like a large, irregular dome, which is very thin and more developed at the back than at the front. Thus, contrary to the impression that you may get from the illustrations, the diaphragm is *not* a rigid dome.

Its edges are attached to the internal outline of the rib cage.

The right half is slightly more curved and higher than the left, especially during a strong exhalation.

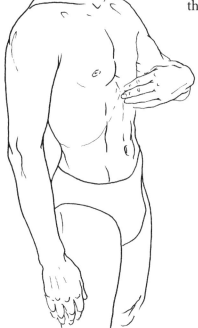

Where in the trunk is the diaphragm located?

The top of the dome is situated at the level of the 4TH or 5TH rib, or slightly higher than the xiphoid process.

At the back, the top is at the level of the 7TH thoracic vertebra. (These are average measurements, and may vary depending on the position of the rib cage and the extent of inhalation and exhalation.)

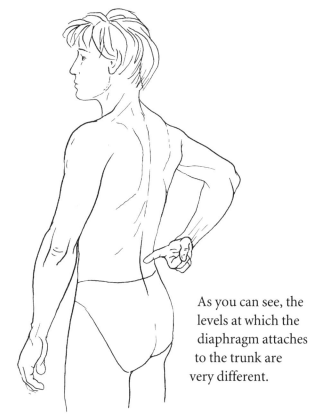

The base of the diaphragm is formed at the back by tendons, which insert into the 3RD lumbar vertebra. This corresponds to the level of the waist.

As you can see, the levels at which the diaphragm attaches to the trunk are very different.

Anatomy of the diaphragm

The diaphragm has a fibrous center part, which is called the *central tendon,* around which are *muscular fibers* arranged in a beam-like fashion. These fibers attach to the entire circumference of the rib cage.

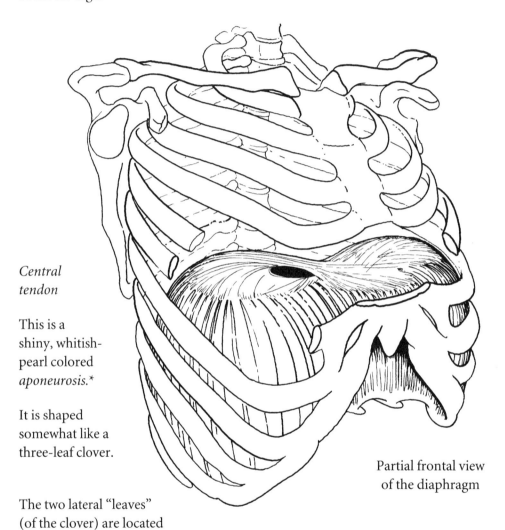

Central tendon

This is a shiny, whitish-pearl colored *aponeurosis.**

It is shaped somewhat like a three-leaf clover.

Partial frontal view of the diaphragm

The two lateral "leaves" (of the clover) are located more posterior and on each side of an indentation, which corresponds to the spinal column. The middle "leaf" is anterior and located behind the sternum.

....

*An aponeurosis is a flexible fibrous tissue that contains numerous collagen fibers which resist pulling. They are arranged in many different directions. An aponeurosis *does not consist of muscular fibers.* Thus, the central tendon is a part of the diaphragm which cannot contract by itself, but is pulled along when the other muscular fibers of the circumference contract. This area passes on the pulling action to other organs that are further away.

Muscular fibers

Muscular fibers originate at the central tendon. They then head down while flaring out and joining the circumference of the rib cage. They form a circular arch, which gives the diaphragm its dome-like shape.

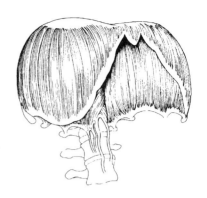

These fibers have different names depending on where they attach:

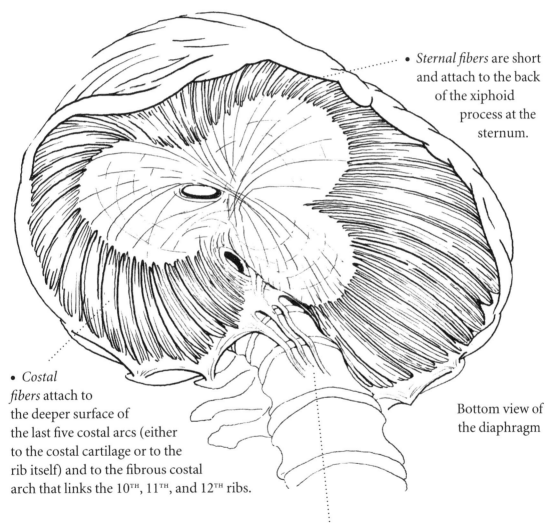

• *Sternal fibers* are short and attach to the back of the xiphoid process at the sternum.

• *Costal fibers* attach to the deeper surface of the last five costal arcs (either to the costal cartilage or to the rib itself) and to the fibrous costal arch that links the 10TH, 11TH, and 12TH ribs.

Bottom view of the diaphragm

• *Vertebral fibers* end at the first three lumbar vertebrae in an asymmetrical fashion. These are called the *pillars* of the diaphragm.

Diaphragm and thoracic organs

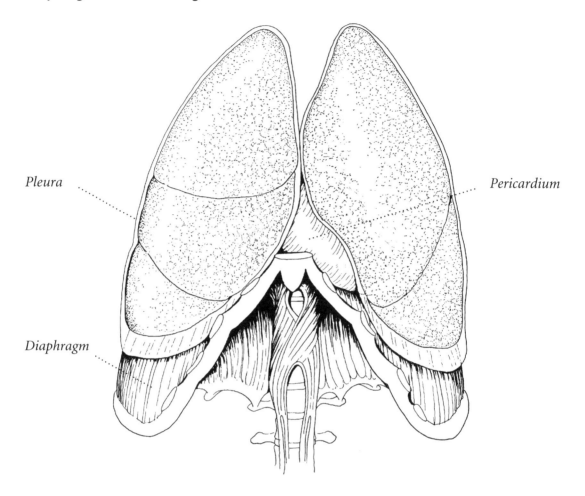

Pleura

Pericardium

Diaphragm

The diaphragm forms a rounded base for the thorax.

The bases of the lungs, which are wrapped in their pleurae, rest on the diaphragm. Thus, the inferior portions of the lungs attach to the superior surface of the diaphragm.

Every movement or deformation of the diaphragm will be transmitted to the base of the lungs (see page 134).

The parietal pleura is larger than the lungs, and the diaphragm drops lower than the pleura. This results in three levels, from bottom to top, as follows: the inferior sides of the diaphragm, the pleura, and the lungs.

The heart rests on the central tendon and is wrapped in a serous membrane, the pericardium. The pericardium, in turn, adheres to the diaphragm at its outer wall and leaves an imprint on the central tendon.

Diaphragm and abdominal organs

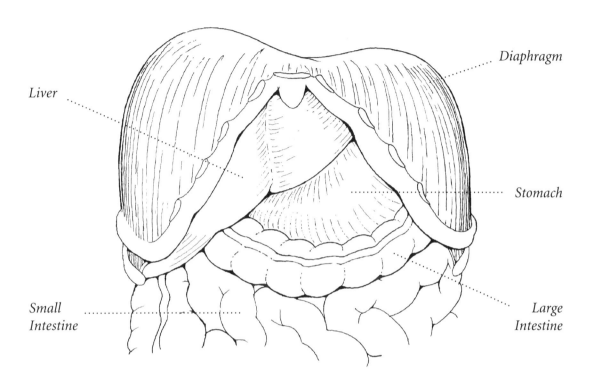

Liver · *Diaphragm*

Stomach

Small Intestine · *Large Intestine*

The diaphragm drapes like a blanket over the upper abdominal organs, partially touching them. It is in contact with some of them through the peritoneum, a great serous envelope, which wraps most of the abdominal organs:

- The stomach (at the left) attaches to the diaphragm on its lateral and partially on its anterior surface.

- The liver attaches to it on its lateral, superior, and posterior surfaces.

The structures behind the peritoneum have direct contact with the diaphragm. These are the kidneys, spleen, pancreas, the abdominal aorta, and the flexures of the large intestine.

Every time the diaphragm moves, it will directly influence the organs, either individually or as a unit, by changing their shape.

Yet even further away, the diaphragm can influence the shape and movement of other organs contained in the abdominal cavity.

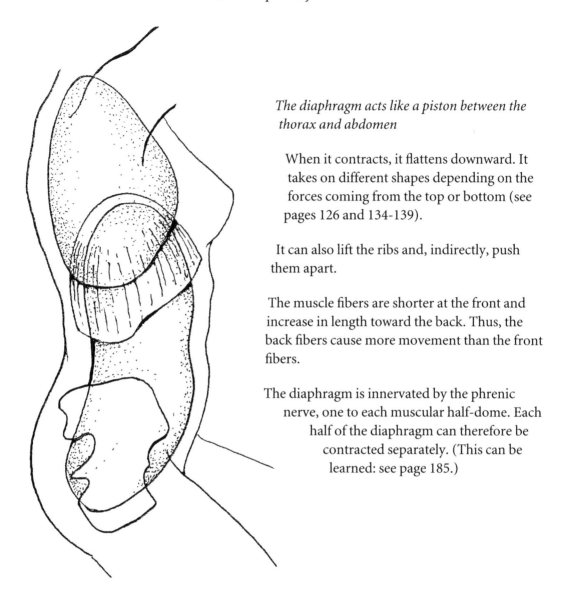

The diaphragm acts like a piston between the thorax and abdomen

When it contracts, it flattens downward. It takes on different shapes depending on the forces coming from the top or bottom (see pages 126 and 134-139).

It can also lift the ribs and, indirectly, push them apart.

The muscle fibers are shorter at the front and increase in length toward the back. Thus, the back fibers cause more movement than the front fibers.

The diaphragm is innervated by the phrenic nerve, one to each muscular half-dome. Each half of the diaphragm can therefore be contracted separately. (This can be learned: see page 185.)

Feeling the contraction of the diaphragm is not easy

The contraction occurs in the middle of the visceral cavity. In addition, it does not have many sensory innervations. There are some nerve fibers coming from the last six intercostal nerves and also from the solar plexus. This is why it is much harder to perceive the muscle contraction of the diaphragm than the contraction of the inspiratory muscles of the rib cage.

One can often feel the movements of the organs, especially the pleurae, which have a lot of sensory nerve endings, without being able to distinguish them clearly from the contractile sensation of the diaphragm. This partly explains why diaphragmatic breathing, although it is the most common and most efficient type of breathing, is not the most easily "felt" type of breathing, especially when practiced consciously and voluntarily.

OTHER MUSCLES OF INSPIRATION OF THE RIB CAGE

Even though normal breathing is usually done through the action of the diaphragm, you can also inhale with the help of other muscles, by "opening" the rib cage with its *muscles of inspiration.*

While the diaphragm works on the interior of the body, the muscles of inspiration of the rib cage work on the outside.

The action of these muscles is much more observable because they are all superficial muscles that can be palpated through the skin: *They are much easier to feel.*

This is why inhalation via the muscles of the rib cage is the first respiratory movement that a beginner can "find," even though this way of breathing is neither the most efficient nor the most common way of inhaling.

It is nevertheless very important to practice this type of inhalation in order to increase the range of spontaneous breathing and also to vary the effects on the rib cage and thoracic region.

On the following pages, you will get to know three groups of muscles of inspiration in the rib cage:

- those that lift the ribs *from the scapular girdle and arm:* pectoralis minor, pectoralis major, and serratus anterior

- those that lift the ribs *from the thoracic spine:* levatores costarum, serratus posterior superior, and (indirectly) the transversospinalis muscles

- those that lift the ribs *from the head and neck:* scalenes, sternocleidomastoid (SCM), and serratus posterior superior.

Some of these muscles help to inhale more laterally, and others more longitudinally (see page 48); they also act on different levels.

Muscles that lift the ribs from the scapular girdle

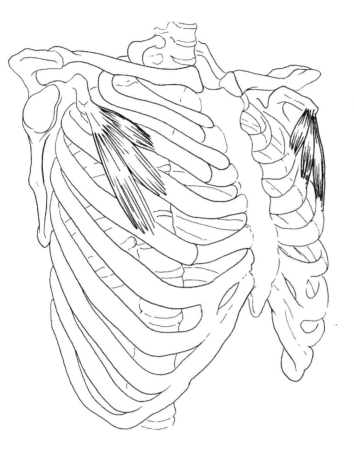

Pectoralis minor

The shoulder blade has a small protuberance which points forward, the *coracoid process*, which is where the pectoralis minor inserts. This muscle runs downward and inward in a fan-like manner and attaches to the 3RD through 5TH ribs.

When this muscle contracts, it lifts the ribs forward. This is the muscle which is moved when inhaling "into the clavicles." This is done by raising the top part of the chest.

This type of inhalation is practically nonexistent in people who are stooped over or whose shoulders are bent forward. In these cases, it is often necessary to first restore the original suppleness to the pectoralis minor (see page 170).

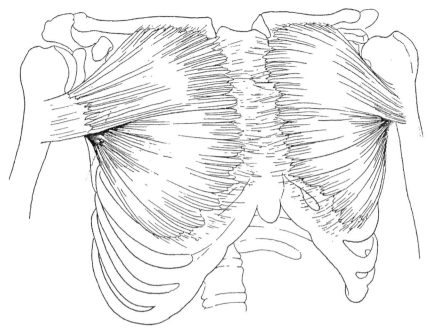

Pectoralis major

This muscle inserts at the top of the arm and drapes over the pectoralis minor, covering it completely. It attaches to the clavicle, the first eight ribs, and the sternum.

The ribs are lifted mostly via the lower muscle fibers attached to ribs 4 through 8. This movement raises the sternum by opening the lower angle of the ribs (costal angle).

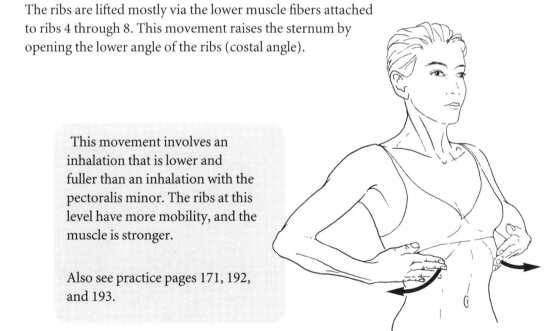

This movement involves an inhalation that is lower and fuller than an inhalation with the pectoralis minor. The ribs at this level have more mobility, and the muscle is stronger.

Also see practice pages 171, 192, and 193.

Serratus anterior

This is a very large muscle which spreads over the entire side of the rib cage. It comes from the shoulder blade, where it attaches to the internal scapular edge, glides over its deep surface without attachment, and skirts the thorax. It then forms a layer which runs parallel to the ribs toward the front and inserts with increasingly long, serrated insertions into ribs 1 through 10.

The serratus anterior lifts the ribs through its five lowest attachments, which pulls the ribs backward and outward, as if to open them up. But since they can't actually "open," the effect is to raise the ribs in a very large, lateral movement, like a bucket handle inhalation. This strongly opens the costal angle (see page 48).

The serratus anterior is one of the most powerful muscles of inspiration. It is often used in singing or when playing a wind instrument, especially for slowing down the pace of exhalation.

The advantage of using this muscle is that it does not involve the neck (with which it has no attachments) but establishes a very firm rib cage posture which serves as a base for the neck region.

Muscles that lift the ribs away from the thoracic spine

Levatores costarum

These are very small but also very numerous muscles which, as a whole, form a large contractile zone.

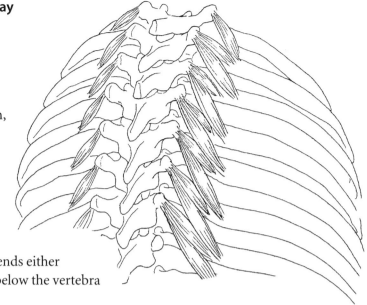

They originate at the transverse process of each of the thoracic vertebrae. Then they collect into a bunch, which descends laterally and ends either one or two ribs immediately below the vertebra from which they originated.

These little bunches all work together to lift the ribs away from the spine. This lifting action occurs at the back of the ribs. These are the muscles involved in inhaling "at the back of the ribs."

At the same time, however, since they attach to the posterior angle of the rib, they also rotate the ribs around themselves like a crank: the proximal portion of the rib lifts up, while the rest of the rib curve drops down. This is a movement of expiration.

In fact, each of these two actions, one of inspiration and the other of expiration, occurs more or less depending on how the other muscles work alongside. For example, if you want to inhale into the entire circumference of the rib cage — front, sides, and back — with a large costal inspiratory reserve volume, you would let the inspiratory movement of the levatores costarum muscles dominate.

Conversely, if you want to completely exhale by contracting the muscle layers that descend from the front of the ribs (rectus abdominis), this expiratory movement can be strengthened by the "expiratory crank motion" of the levatores costarum muscles.

Transversospinalis muscles:
indirect inhalation muscles

These posterior muscles lie in thick layers along the spinal vertebrae. Their principal function is to *extend the spine*.

The extension of the thoracic spine most often leads to a forward lifting of the rib cage, which is an action of inhalation.

Consequently, these muscles are considered to be indirect participants in the action of inhalation.

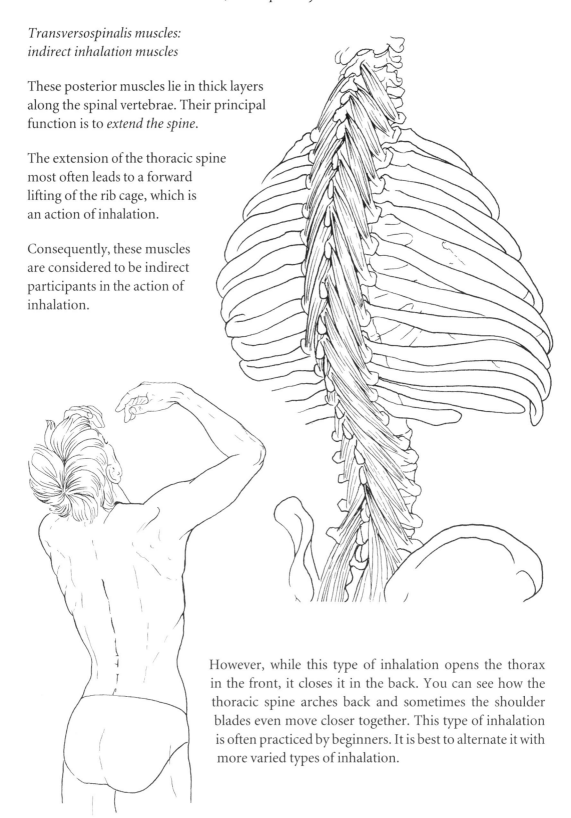

However, while this type of inhalation opens the thorax in the front, it closes it in the back. You can see how the thoracic spine arches back and sometimes the shoulder blades even move closer together. This type of inhalation is often practiced by beginners. It is best to alternate it with more varied types of inhalation.

Serratus posterior superior

This muscle originates at the spinous processes of C7 and T1 through T3/4. It forms a small layer which descends outward and inserts into the first four or five ribs at the level of the posterior costal angle.

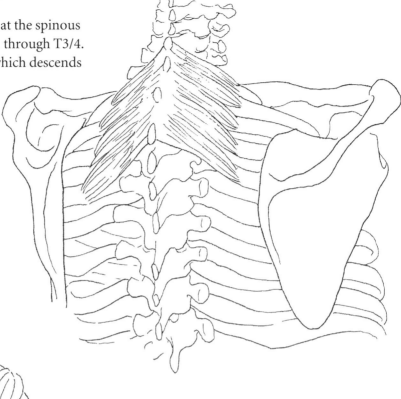

It can lift the ribs from the vertebrae, to which it is attached, and thus participates in the inhalation "into the back" of the higher ribs. Thus, it completes at the top the action of the levatores costarum.

However, at this level the ribs are short and not very mobile, minimizing the respiratory movements. Nevertheless, the muscle is relevant for mobilizing this area at the vertebral and costal levels.

Muscles that lift the ribs from the head or neck

Sternocleidomastoid

The sternocleidomastoid (SCM) is a very prominent muscle at the front of the neck. It sits directly under the skin, and fibers from the pair of SCM muscles form the "V" shape which extends from the region under the ears to the upper part of the sternum.

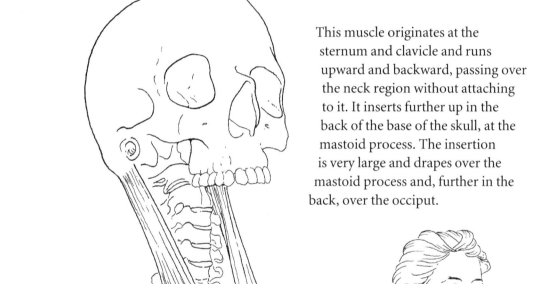

This muscle originates at the sternum and clavicle and runs upward and backward, passing over the neck region without attaching to it. It inserts further up in the back of the base of the skull, at the mastoid process. The insertion is very large and drapes over the mastoid process and, further in the back, over the occiput.

The SCM raises the rib cage by pulling it upward at the top of the sternum. Thus, it contributes to a very high inhalation.

Scalenes

These muscles extend from the cervical spine to the first two ribs. There are three different scalene muscles: scalenus anterior, scalenus medius, and scalenus posterior.

They are attached to the transverse process of the cervical vertebrae and descend slightly outward and forward.

Scalenus anterior and scalenus medius insert at the first rib. The scalenus posterior inserts at the second rib.

The scalenes can raise the first and second ribs and thus participate in very high rib breathing.

These muscles raise the edges of the ribs, which gives them a more lateral pull than the SCM.

This nuance is, however, not very significant at this rib level since the movements here, especially the lateral ones, are minimal. We can say that the scalene muscles as a whole contribute to very high respiratory movements.

The cervical spine offers a fixed point at the higher insertion of these muscles so that they can raise the ribs. However, the cervical region is the least stable region of the entire spine because of the small size of the vertebrae and the great mobility of the cervical spine. Therefore, the spine must be fixed and stabilized, either by use of a headrest or by resting on the floor, or by using the muscles which can fix the spine, especially the long anterior neck muscles.

MUSCLES OF EXPIRATION

Remember that the first expiratory force is the elasticity of the lungs themselves. This force is responsible for most of the act of exhalation.

The muscles of expiration are involved in:

- increasing the expiratory reserve volume

- accentuating the force of exhalation (e.g., when blowing up a balloon)

- accelerating the rate of exhalation.

These muscles assist in reducing the volume of the lungs. To do this, they either drop the ribs, raise up the base of the lungs, or do both at the same time. (For more detail, see pages 146-149).

Abdominal muscles

These muscles support and surround the abdomen. There are four of them on the left and on the right:

- the *rectus abdominis* in the front

- three layers of large muscles that lay on top of each other on the sides.

Relative to the abdomen, the abdominal muscles *mobilize the organs* in a number of ways. They can lift them up and thus participate in expiration. This is their "visceral" action.

Relative to the skeleton, the abdominal muscles *move the spine, pelvis, and especially the ribs* in an expiratory direction. This is their "skeletal" action.

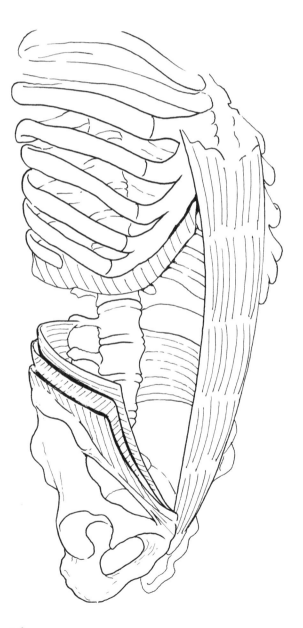

*Transversus abdominis:
partner of the diaphragm*

This muscle attaches at the top to the deep
surface of the lower rib cage. At the back,
it is attached via a fibrous sheet to the
lumbar vertebrae at the bottom, to the
iliac crest, and the inguinal ligament.

These muscle fibers surround the sides
of the abdomen like a belt, then change
into a large fibrous area in the front.
This is the anterior aponeurosis of the
transversus abdominis. The right and left
aponeuroses unite in the middle anterior
portion via a region of crisscrossing fibers
called *linea alba*.

Contraction of the transversus abdominis
reduces the diameter of the abdomen. Of
all the abdominal muscles, this is the one
whose action is the most visceral. Its action
does not really affect the skeleton, however.
In a lot of movements, it acts in combination
with the diaphragm (see pages 148 and 149).

This is the muscle that helps you "narrow your waist." This
action is greatest at the level of the costoiliac region where its
fibers are the biggest. It is not good for the muscle to be the
dominant participant here, because it exerts a strong pressure on
the lower part of the abdomen. That is why it is often necessary to
coordinate its action with other abdominal muscles.

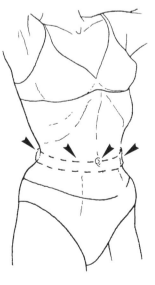

Obliques: two crisscrossing layers

Internal oblique

This muscle attaches at the top to the lower rib cage and at the bottom to the iliac crest and the inguinal ligament.

Its fibers travel from the back to the front across the sides of the waist and then change to a broad fibrous area anteriorly, called the anterior aponeurosis of the internal oblique.

At the bottom, the fibers of the internal oblique run parallel to the inguinal ligament to the pubic crest. They converge with some of the fibers of the transversus abdominis along the groin.

Among other actions, the internal oblique participates in expiration in the following ways:

- It participates in costal expiration by lowering the ribs.

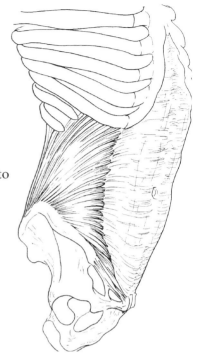

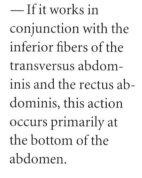

- It reduces the diameter of the abdomen.

— If it works in conjunction with the transversus abdominis, this action occurs primarily at the waist.

— If it works in conjunction with the inferior fibers of the transversus abdominis and the rectus abdominis, this action occurs primarily at the bottom of the abdomen.

The lower fibers of the internal oblique (mostly), transverse abdominis, and rectus abdominis form the "lower" abdominal muscles. After the muscles of the pelvic floor, these muscle fibers are the ones that begin the contraction of the abdomen in the rising abdominal expiration (see page 149).

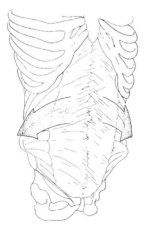

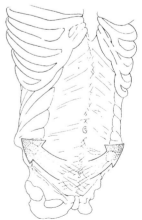

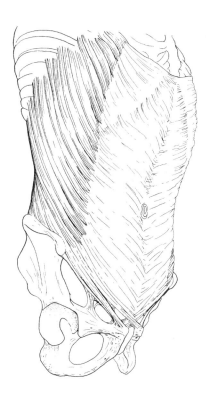

External oblique

This muscle attaches at the top to the outside of the lower rib cage and at the bottom to the iliac crest and the inguinal ligament.

The muscle fibers travel from the back to the front across the sides of the trunk and then change to a broad fibrous area called the anterior aponeurosis of the external oblique.

Among many other actions, the external oblique participates in expiration in the following ways:

- It participates in costal expiration by lowering the ribs.

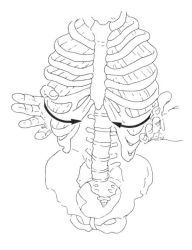

- It reduces the diameter of the abdomen, when working in conjunction with the transversus abdominis. In this case, the action occurs primarily at the waist.

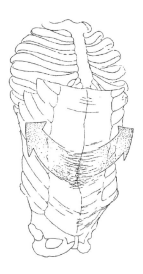

- It pulls in the lowest part of the abdomen (via its lowest fibers) when working in conjunction with the rectus abdominis and the lower fibers of the transverse abdominis.

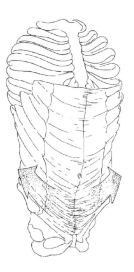

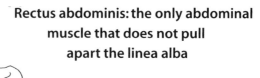

Rectus abdominis: the only abdominal muscle that does not pull apart the linea alba

At the top, this muscle attaches to the sternum and the costal cartilage of ribs 5-7, and at the bottom to the pubic crest.

Its muscle fibers run downward lengthwise at the front of the abdomen. They are interrupted and alternated by aponeurotic areas, which give the muscle its characteristic square shapes.

Among other actions, the rectus abdominis participates in expiration in the following ways:

• It participates in anterior costal expiration by dropping the sternum.

• It participates in intensive expirations by raising the pubic bone (an action used sometimes for totally closing the anterior abdomen).

• It completes the rectus sheath of the other large abdominal muscles. The advantage of using the rectus abdominis is that it pulls without pulling the abdomen apart, as do the other large abdominal muscles. This is a good muscle to use when "sucking in the stomach" during expiration (think of doing this action "from the front").

The rectus abdominis always participates at the beginning of each exhalation by using its lowest fibers (in conjunction with those of the other abdominal muscles) to hold and suck in the lowest, most anterior portion of the abdomen.

Pelvic floor: the foundation of breathing

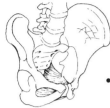

All the muscles at the bottom of the pelvis are called the pelvic floor. They form the lowest portion of the trunk. The pelvic floor consists of two layers:

- a superficial layer at the bottom (not shown in detail here, because it does not play an important role in breathing)

- a deep layer located above it in the lesser pelvis. This layer contains the levator ani and the ischiococcygeus muscles. This deep layer has the shape and size of a bowl.

Levator ani

This muscle attaches to the circumference of the lesser pelvis, along a line extending from the pubis to the ischial spine and the midsection of the sacrum. In men, the anterior portion of this muscle is closed: this is the *scrotal floor*. In women, there is an indentation at this area, the *urogenital groove,* which extends into the vulva.

Ischiococcygeus

This muscle runs from the ischial spine to the sacrum and coccyx. Its posterior extent completes the bowl shape.

How are these muscles involved in breathing?

They do not play a dynamic part in expiration: since their surface is very small, they cannot cause a big movement with every contraction. Nor can they lift the big abdominal mass with the efficiency of the muscles discussed in previous pages, as some would suggest.

Still, this area of the pelvic floor is the base of the abdominal cavity, for which it serves as:

- a contractile foundation that must be able to *adapt its tonicity* so that it is neither too high nor too low in order to withstand the deep pushing action it endures during inhalation and exhalation

- a foundation that will initiate the successive "rising" muscle contractions of the abdominal cavity in connection with certain expiratory actions (see page 149).

Expiratory muscles that move the ribs

Transversus thoracis at the inside of the rib cage

This is an unusual muscle because it is located at the inside of the rib cage. It originates from the posterior surface of the sternum, and its fibers are arranged like a fan and insert on the cartilages of ribs 2 through 7.

When contracting, it lowers the costal cartilages and moves them backward, thus closing the region around the sternum.

This is a muscle of expiration which sits very anterior, yet its contraction occurs in the depth of the rib cage. It is easy to feel this movement when coughing.

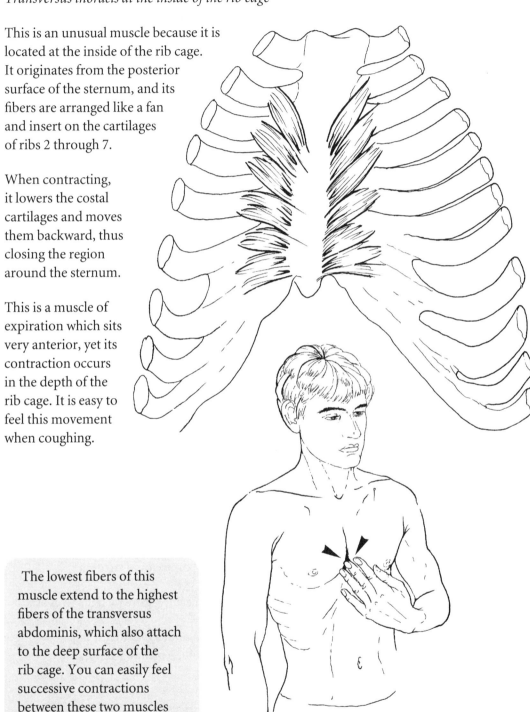

The lowest fibers of this muscle extend to the highest fibers of the transversus abdominis, which also attach to the deep surface of the rib cage. You can easily feel successive contractions between these two muscles (see page 211).

Quadratus lumborum

This muscle originates from the iliac crest and inserts on rib 12 and the transverse processes of the lumbar vertebrae.

Contraction of this muscle lowers rib 12, and thus it participates in expiration.

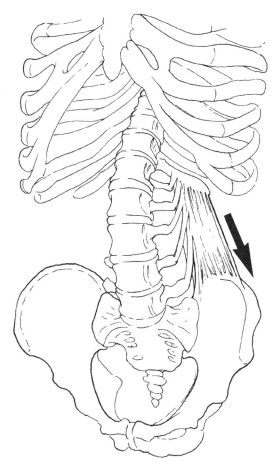

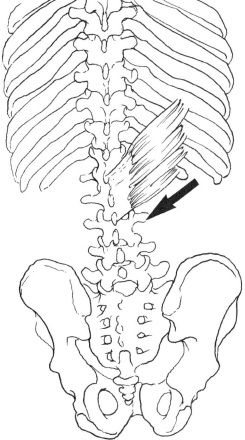

Serratus posterior inferior

This muscle runs from the higher lumbar vertebrae (L1-L2) and lower thoracic vertebrae (T10-12) to ribs 9-12.

Contraction of this muscle lowers these ribs, and thus it participates in expiration.

These two muscles work in posterior breathing. If you make these muscles work in costal expiration, the resulting exhalation will be felt as a movement in the back of the waist. An example is breathing with a "rounded belly" (see page 215).

Respiratory muscles with variable actions

Intercostals — inspiratory muscles

The intercostal muscles occupy the spaces between adjacent ribs and are arranged in two crisscrossing layers.

External intercostals

These have fibers that run obliquely downward and forward.

Internal intercostals

These have fibers that run obliquely downward and backward.

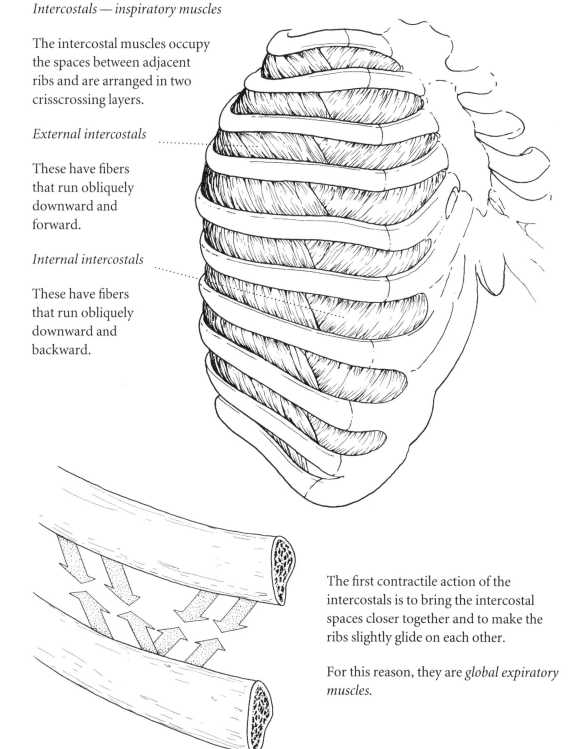

The first contractile action of the intercostals is to bring the intercostal spaces closer together and to make the ribs slightly glide on each other.

For this reason, they are *global expiratory muscles.*

This action, however, can change totally, depending on where the ribs are fixed.

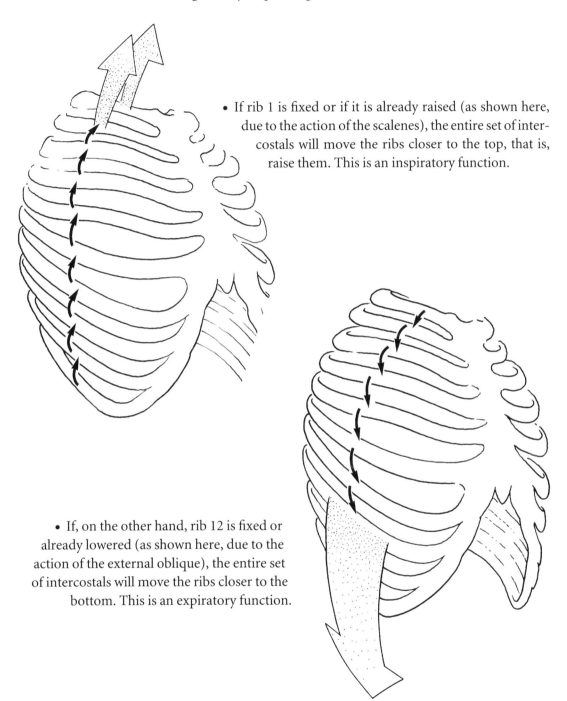

- If rib 1 is fixed or if it is already raised (as shown here, due to the action of the scalenes), the entire set of intercostals will move the ribs closer to the top, that is, raise them. This is an inspiratory function.

- If, on the other hand, rib 12 is fixed or already lowered (as shown here, due to the action of the external oblique), the entire set of intercostals will move the ribs closer to the bottom. This is an expiratory function.

We can therefore see that these muscles generally work in static contraction; the set of muscles forms a layer, connecting the ribs to each other. Thus, a movement occurring at one rib will be followed by movement in the neighboring ribs, or even by the entire rib cage.

. . . .

CHAPTER FIVE

The Principal Forces
Involved in Breathing

THE BREATHING ACTIONS described on pages 18 through 21 can be made with the involvement of many different forces. We have seen, on pages 70 through 105, that many different muscles can contribute to inhalation, exhalation, and apnea (cessation of breathing). However, the actions of these muscles are not always due to their contraction, but sometimes to other factors.

In brief, the actions of the muscles combine with many other forces, any one of which may sometimes be the main force in the act of breathing. Among these forces are gravity, the response to supporting structures (headrest, floor, etc.), the elasticity of the lungs, and even the rigidity of the skeleton (resisting movement).

This chapter will take a look at the most common forces and how they combine in various situations.

MUSCLES ACT IN DIFFERENT WAYS DURING BREATHING

1. They contract to produce a breathing action.

This is called concentric contraction.

For example, the contraction of the pectoralis major raises the ribs, and thus *produces* an anterior costal inhalation.

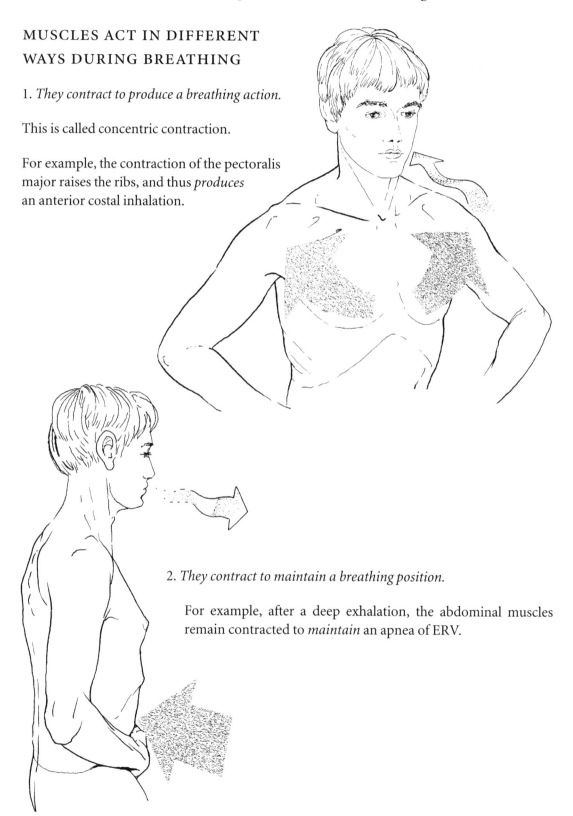

2. They contract to maintain a breathing position.

For example, after a deep exhalation, the abdominal muscles remain contracted to *maintain* an apnea of ERV.

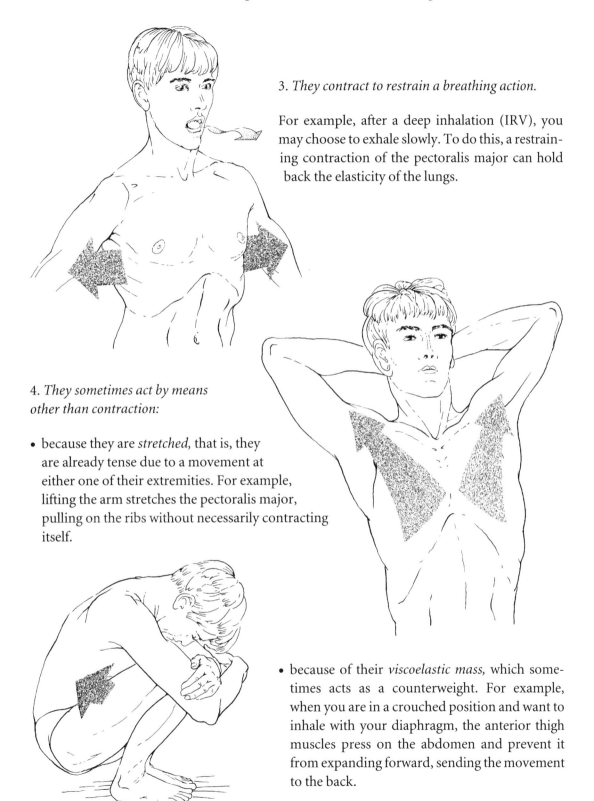

3. *They contract to restrain a breathing action.*

For example, after a deep inhalation (IRV), you may choose to exhale slowly. To do this, a restraining contraction of the pectoralis major can hold back the elasticity of the lungs.

4. *They sometimes act by means other than contraction:*

• because they are *stretched,* that is, they are already tense due to a movement at either one of their extremities. For example, lifting the arm stretches the pectoralis major, pulling on the ribs without necessarily contracting itself.

• because of their *viscoelastic mass,* which sometimes acts as a counterweight. For example, when you are in a crouched position and want to inhale with your diaphragm, the anterior thigh muscles press on the abdomen and prevent it from expanding forward, sending the movement to the back.

PULMONARY ELASTICITY: AN IMPORTANT FORCE IN BREATHING

We have seen on page 61 that, from a mechanical standpoint, the lungs behave like a rubber band. More than a string, they are like a rubber band in three dimensions, like playing cat's cradle.

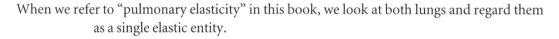

The lungs allow for a certain opening movement when a force from the outside stretches them. This is called pulmonary expansion. But at the same time, they resist this type of stretching, and as soon as the force ends, they return to their original shape.

When we refer to "pulmonary elasticity" in this book, we look at both lungs and regard them as a single elastic entity.

Elasticity in "3-D"

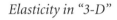

One way to visualize the elasticity of the lungs is to take a kitchen glove and try to stretch it apart. To see how this works in the body, ask a few people to pull each finger of the glove in a different direction.

With two hands, stretch the glove apart, one hand pulling upward, the other downward. This vertical aspect of pulmonary elasticity causes a resistance which tries to pull the first hand downward and the second upward. This is how to visualize the elastic action between the top of the rib cage and the base of the rib cage (the diaphragm).

With two hands, stretch the glove sideways. This is the resistance of the lungs when they are subjected to lateral pulling forces. This is how to visualize the elastic action of the lungs between the lateral walls of the rib cage.

Now use one hand to pull the glove forward and the other to pull it backward (not shown here). This is how to visualize further resistance of the lungs, which will take the first hand backward and the second forward.

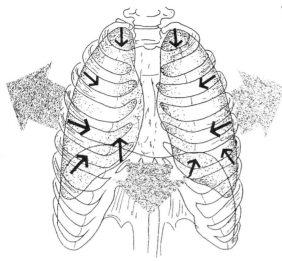

The lungs resist inhalation

In most breathing actions, a certain force must be applied to open and stretch the lungs, since they resist such stretching. It can therefore be said that the lungs, elastically speaking, more or less resist an inhalation depending on the respiratory volume (see pages 118 and 120).

This is often visualized as the lungs being the force that opens the rib cage.

The lungs as the primary force of expiration

Most exhalations are caused by the elasticity of the lungs.

Thus, the force applied to expiration is mostly an elastic force, rather than a muscular one. This, of course, is more or less true depending on the respiratory volume involved (see pages 117 and 123). However, this elastic force alone cannot completely empty the lungs. When, because of their elasticity, they return to their original shape, they still have a lot of air inside. This is the residual volume (RV).

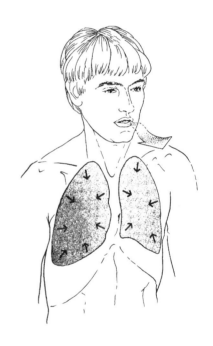

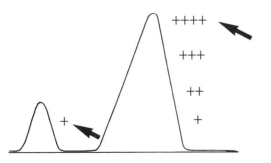

The elastic force of the lungs varies.

The force that returns the lungs to their original shape is very powerful, especially when the lungs are stretched. For example, it is more powerful after an IRV than after an inhalation of tidal volume.

This force of elastic recoil also contributes indirectly to many other actions that are unrelated to breathing. It can, for example, suck in the belly, mobilize the organs, pull in the ribs, bend the lumbar vertebrae, or bend the cervical region.

Gravity: another factor in breathing

Gravity has a different effect on the respiratory structure, depending on the position of the body. Sometimes it favors inhalation, sometimes exhalation. Here, we will look at gravity with respect to the diaphragm and the rib cage.

1. Gravity and the diaphragm

Recall that the diaphragm is "glued" to the abdominal organs through the peritoneum.

When it contracts, the diaphragm tends to move toward the pelvis. Gravity affects the abdominal mass like it would a "water balloon" which moves in different directions depending on the position of the body.

A. The "water balloon" moves in the same direction as the diaphragm.

When a person is standing, for example, the abdomen is situated below the diaphragm and does not oppose its descent. Gravity works in the same direction as the diaphragm. It moves in an inspiratory direction.

B. Sometimes the "water balloon" moves the diaphragm further than it would move on its own when contracting.

This happens when the abdominal muscles are not contracted and the visceral mass moves forward out of the abdominal cavity.

For example, when you kneel on all fours and relax the abdominal muscles, the abdomen moves toward the floor and pulls the diaphragm with it.

Another example is when you stand and totally relax the abdominal muscles. In this case, the "water balloon" falls toward the front and moves the diaphragm, which then descends passively.

In this case, inhalation is passive and the weight of the abdomen opposes expiration.

This is one of two cases where inhalation is not produced through a muscular contraction. (The second case is explained on page 123).

This is used as a technique in singing, for quick inhalations of air after a forced exhalation in ERV.

It also occurs when a person has a very big belly. The protruding belly pulls the diaphragm along with it, even the entire rib cage.

C. Sometimes the "water balloon" bears down on the diaphragm.

For example, in a headstand, the diaphragm must counter the weight of the abdominal organs in order to move toward the pelvis. In this case, it has to work much more intensely.

In a side-lying position, the abdominal "water balloon" bears down less directly. It weighs down on the half of the diaphragm that is resting on the floor.

2. Gravity and the rib cage

When standing, gravity makes the ribs *drop.* Thus, it acts in an expiratory fashion. This is the most common effect of gravity on the rib cage.

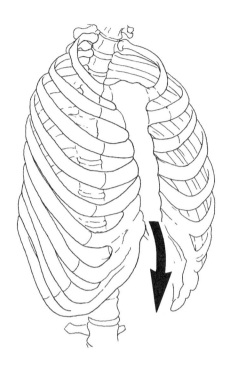

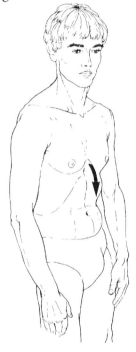

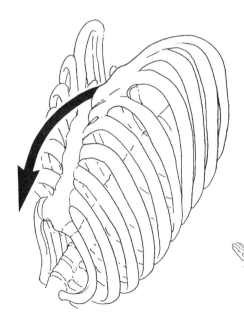

On the other hand, when the head is positioned lower than the trunk, it causes the ribs to raise up. Thus, it acts in an inspiratory fashion.

As you can see, when gravity pulls the diaphragm into an expiratory action (by pushing it toward the top of the thorax, as on the previous page), it pulls the ribs into an inspiratory movement (as is the case here). *Gravity thus frequently acts in opposite directions on the ribs and the diaphragm.*

The skeleton: another factor in breathing

The skeleton acts through its rigidity, which is more or less complete with respect to the respiratory system, in conjunction with several other forces:

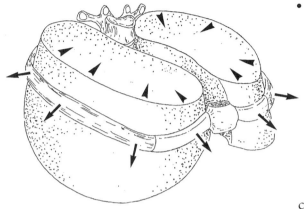

- The costal arch is semi-rigid and opposes the elastic force of the lungs.

  - The ribs are also semi-rigid and serve to relay the pulling forces of the inspiratory and expiratory muscles and point them in specific directions.

  - The semi-rigidity of the spinal column affects the movements of the trunk and of the rib cage, and consequently of breathing actions.

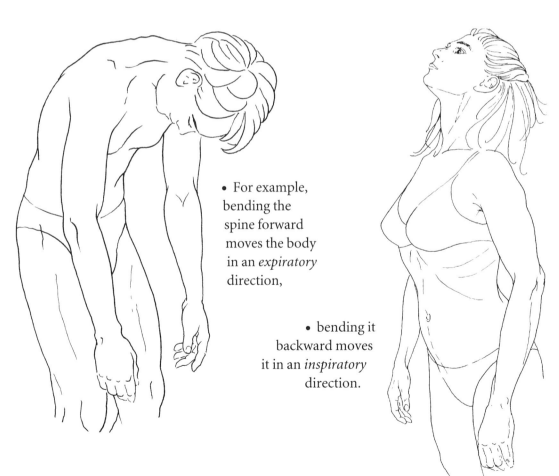

- For example, bending the spine forward moves the body in an *expiratory* direction,

- bending it backward moves it in an *inspiratory* direction.

CHAPTER SIX

....

Forces Affecting Respiratory Volumes

WHY ARE SOME inhalations passive and others active? How can apnea occur both during a time of total relaxation and of intense activity?

Depending on the time it takes to breathe or the volume of a breath, the forces involved in these actions can change completely.

To understand what happens in different types of breathing, it is important to observe how *the principal forces act differently depending on the volume.*

We will look closely at the forces and how they act with respect to each respiratory volume during inhalation, exhalation, and apnea.

Without even realizing it, we often thread together several of the volumes described on pages 25-29 into one act of breathing, passing seamlessly from one force to another as we breathe.

It is therefore advisable to *read through the following pages very thoroughly and assimilate their contents* so that you can later "play" with the forces, readily identifying them at each volume and in each movement. It is best if you can recognize these forces in real time, at the same rate at which you are performing the respective act of breathing.

The analysis in the following pages refers to breathing in a standing position, at a normal rate, without accelerating or slowing down.

FORCES INVOLVED IN BREATHING OF TIDAL VOLUME

1. Inhaling tidal volume

During inhalation, you use the inspiratory muscles, which open the lungs as they contract.*

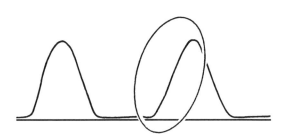

At this small volume, the diaphragm is usually the only muscle that is working (see page 134). In this case, you especially open the *base* of the lungs.

Inhalation does not involve many muscles, and those that are involved are not required to do very much. It is not important that many muscles be used, or that they act forcefully, because the action is so small.

This type of inhalation slightly stretches the elasticity of the lungs, which progressively accumulates a little more elastic recoil force. The expiratory muscles are relaxed.

In summary, the forces involved here are:

- moderate muscle contraction of inspiratory muscle
- relaxation of expiratory muscles
- slight stretching of the pulmonary elasticity.

If you were to stop breathing (apnea) during this type of inhalation:

The inspiratory muscles would stay contracted (static), without any muscular movement. They would keep the lungs in their expanded position. From a muscular standpoint, this would be an *active* apnea.

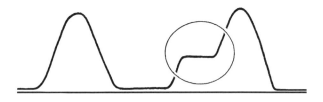

....

*When you are standing, this may just be the force of gravity (see page 113).

2. Exhaling tidal volume

The pulmonary elasticity, which is slightly stretched, causes the lungs to return to their original shape. Air is moved out of the lungs, but not entirely. What remains is the volume of ERV and RV.

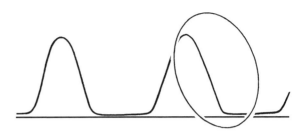

The inspiratory muscles relax. (We will, however, qualify this notion on page 121.)

The expiratory muscles do not work during this type of exhalation.

This is important to remember: Exhalation of tidal volume does not require any work for the expiratory muscles, contrary to what is often thought. Thus, it is a very *relaxed* exhalation.

Exhalation of tidal volume is very compatible with movements of similar quality: relaxation and easy-going movements.

In summary, the forces involved here are:

- elastic returning force of the lungs
- muscular relaxation (as much for the inspiratory as the expiratory muscles).

If you were to stop breathing (apnea) during this type of exhalation:

The inspiratory muscles are statically contracted, that is, there is no muscular movement, and this contraction hinders the lungs from returning to their original shape. The contraction is moderate because the

pulmonary elasticity is not under much tension and only slightly resists the stretching.

If you were to stop breathing (apnea) at the end of this type of exhalation:

The inspiratory muscles have returned to their resting position and the pulmonary elasticity has returned to a position of relaxation.

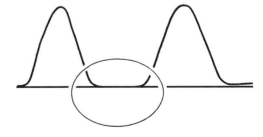

See page 153 for a discussion of the benefits of this movement.

FORCES INVOLVED IN INSPIRATORY RESERVE VOLUME (IRV)

1. Inhaling IRV

The inspiratory muscles "open" the lungs, but in a much stronger manner than in tidal volume. Thus, the inspiratory muscles are involved more prominently in one of the following ways:

- through one inspiratory muscle that works strongly
- through several inspiratory muscles working together
- through a combination of the two.

The pulmonary elasticity is more stretched than in tidal volume.

The expiratory muscles are relaxed to allow for the expansion of the lungs.

As the amplitude of the IRV increases, these phenomena become stronger. As air intake increases:

- The inspiratory muscles work more.
- The tension on the elasticity of the lungs increases.
- The expiratory muscles become more relaxed.

When you inhale a lot of air, these actions are at their maximum. The pulmonary elastic tissue, when under extreme tension, has a very strong elastic recoil force. (This is explored more thoroughly on practice pages 206-207.)

This type of inhalation is compatible with actions of a similar quality: body toning, vigilance, impulsive movements.

In summary, the forces involved here are:

- major work of the inspiratory muscles
- strong stretching of the elastic pulmonary tissue
- relaxation of the expiratory muscles.

If you were to stop breathing (apnea) during inhalation of IRV:

The inspiratory muscles, which up to that point had worked to "open the lungs," will continue to contract to keep them in this open position. They work in static contraction (also called isometric). From a muscular standpoint, this is an *active* apnea, especially when the IRV is really large.

2. Exhaling IRV

The pulmonary elasticity, which was very stretched, returns the lungs to their original shape. This begins with a lot of force as one starts to exhale, then progressively loses force until tidal volume is reached.

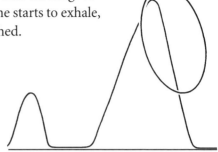

This elastic recoil is large and must be moderated, especially at the beginning of the exhalation from a deep IRV inhalation.

The slow down is accomplished by a *contraction of the muscles that resist expiration, the inspiratory muscles.*

In this case, the inspiratory muscles do not help with inhalation, but instead restrain exhalation. This type of contraction is called "eccentric."

The expiratory muscles, on the other hand, are relaxed. They are not involved in the exhalation when returning from IRV, even if it is forceful.

These actions are more pronounced the deeper the inhalation preceding this movement.

In summary, the forces involved here are:

- a large force to return pulmonary elasticity
- a slowing action by the inspiratory muscles
- relaxation of expiratory muscles.

If you were to stop breathing (apnea) during exhalation of IRV:

The inspiratory muscles, which resisted the pulmonary elasticity, continue to work, but without any movement (static contraction). This contraction is more intense the earlier in the IRV exhalation that it occurs, and the deeper the IRV.

All these types of IRV breathing, and their associated apneas, that were described in these last two pages can be used to *develop stronger inspiratory muscles.*

FORCES INVOLVED IN EXPIRATORY RESERVE VOLUME (ERV)

1. Exhaling ERV

When a breath returns from tidal volume or from an IRV there is still a lot of air in the lungs. Once the lungs have returned to their original shape, this air cannot be expelled through pulmonary elasticity.

To expel more air, your body must *apply expiratory pressure on the lungs*. This pressure is applied through the action of the expiratory muscles in one of the following ways:

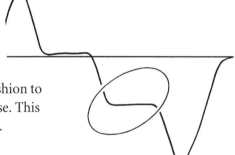

- They lower the ribs even further.
- They raise the abdominal mass more toward the thorax, pushing up the lungs from the base to the top.
- They do both simultaneously (see pages 146-149).

This action becomes more intense as you try to expel more air, in other words, as you increase the amplitude of ERV. At this point, the pulmonary elastic tissue is folded up, even "crumpled" up, instead of being stretched. The rib cage is closed, with the ribs torsioned on themselves.

In summary, the forces involved here are:

- concentric work of expiratory muscles
- compression of pulmonary tissue and resistance to this compression
- ribs dropped down low and torsioned
- relaxation of inspiratory muscles.

If you were to stop breathing (apnea) during exhalation in ERV:

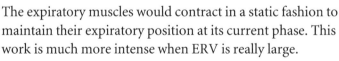

The expiratory muscles would contract in a static fashion to maintain their expiratory position at its current phase. This work is much more intense when ERV is really large.

Expiration of ERV can be used especially to:
- develop expiratory muscle tone
- enable passive inhalation (see following pages).

2. Inhaling ERV

Depending on the intensity of the exhalation, the lungs are compressed and "crumpled" onto themselves, and the ribs are dropped and curved. To inhale from this position, it is enough to relax the muscle contractions, which keeps the lungs compressed and the ribs forcibly curved. This means that the *expiratory muscles must be relaxed.*

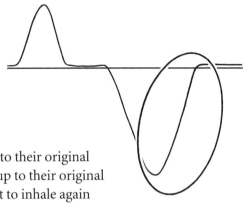

Because of their elasticity, the ribs will then return to their original curvature, and this will cause the lungs to expand up to their original position of tidal volume. These forces are sufficient to inhale again during the entire return amplitude of ERV.*

> This is one of only two cases where inhalation can be done without muscle contraction. This gives the action a "letting go" or "letting breathing happen" quality. This type of inhalation is therefore often used in relaxation techniques (see page 209).

In summary, the forces involved here are:

- relaxation of expiratory muscles
- return of ribs to a less curved position
- return of pulmonary tissue to an uncompressed position
- relaxation of inspiratory muscles.

If you were to stop breathing (apnea) during inhalation in ERV:

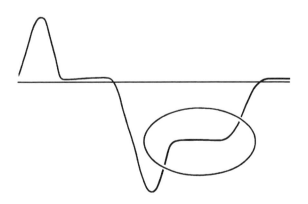

The expiratory muscles would stop relaxing and start contracting statically to prevent the ribs from un-curving and the lungs from filling up again — the respiratory movement is suspended.

> *If you want to inhale more, your inspiratory muscles must work in order to stretch the lungs. This will bring you back to the beginning of tidal volume, described on page 118.

FORCES INVOLVED IN THE RATE OF BREATHING

As we have seen on page 32, all different types of breathing can occur at different rates. This is done by modifying the forces involved.

To accelerate breathing, there are two primary conditions:

- *The airways must be as free of blockage as possible.* The airways can be obstructed for many reasons, including pathological obstructive diseases. They can also be shrunk or cleared, in a more or less conscious and voluntary manner, and at certain locations, such as the glottis, the soft palate, the pharynx, the mouth, and the lips (see page 130 for information on the occlusives).

- *The forces that move the air must be more intense.* Remember that these forces are not limited to muscular contractions.

To slow breathing, there are also two primary conditions:

- *The diameter of the airways can be narrowed* at certain points, such as the glottis, pharynx, mouth, and lips.

- *The forces that affect expiration can be restrained.* You can limit pulmonary elasticity during the return of IRV or tidal volume; you can also moderate the contraction of the expiratory muscles in ERV.

For each of the volumes described on pages 118-123, you can think of forces that could be modified to change the rate of breathing.

....

CHAPTER SEVEN

Relationships Among Anatomical Structures Involved in Breathing

TWO CAVITIES THAT ARE INSEPARABLE DURING BREATHING

Breathing involves specific movements between two cavities, which act very differently:

- the thoracic cavity
- the abdominal cavity.

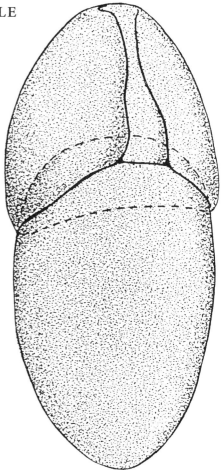

These two enclosures are, at the same time, separated and united by the diaphragm. The thorax is attached to the diaphragm via the pleurae and the pericardium; the abdomen is attached to the diaphragm via the peritoneum. It acts like "double-sided tape" between the two cavities.

At the same time, though, the diaphragm is a deformable, contractile, and elastic wall, just like any other muscle.

These two cavities are indivisible. Even though, from a visceral perspective, the actions of breathing occur only in the thorax, from a functional perspective, it is impossible to dissociate the actions in the thorax from those in the abdomen.

Conversely, movements in the abdomen affect the thorax and thus the breathing. This is why the act of breathing will always deform both cavities at the same time and in many different ways.

This leads to a great variety of breathing situations, and also a great variety of movements that occur using the structures of breathing, but without being respiratory.* Some of these movements will be discussed in the next chapter.

We will take a closer look at the two cavities in order to recognize and understand their anatomical structure, that is, the mechanical characteristics of their *contents* and *containers*.

....

*See "Techniques for decompressing the abdominal organs" on page 150.

Thoracic cavity

What are the contents of this cavity?

Most of it is *air* (in the lungs). The most striking features of air are that it is deformable and elastic, that is, it can be compressed and decompressed. You can thus create high pressure and low pressure in the thoracic cavity.

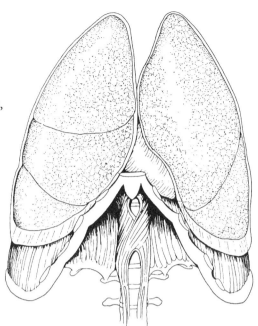

This cavity also contains *pulmonary tissue*, which is also deformable and elastic. This means that the tissue can be stretched and, when released, it will return to its original shape. But if the stretching continues, the resulting force of the elastic recoil will cause the lungs to pull neighboring structures closer.

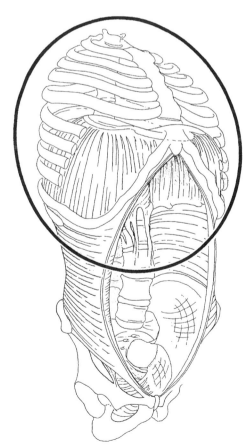

What is the container of this cavity?

The thoracic cavity is located in a bony structure, the rib cage, which is at the same time (and to some extent):

- semi-rigid
- deformable, especially at the bottom
- elastic.

When the rib cage changes due to a change in the costal curvature, and then the force causing this change is removed, the rib cage tends to return to its original shape.

The rib cage is moved by *muscles* that are at the same time contractile and elastic.

Abdominal cavity

What are the contents of this cavity?

The abdominal cavity contains soft organs that can be compared to a *liquid mass*, a "water balloon." These contents are *deformable* but *cannot be compressed.* Any force applied to any part of this "balloon" will cause a deformation somewhere else.

This mechanical aspect is very important. It explains why and how the abdomen moves and is deformed during diaphragmatic breathing.

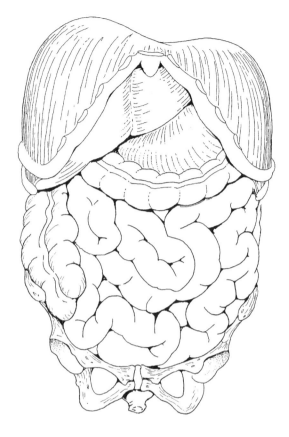

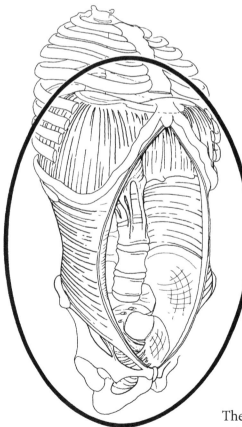

What is the container of this cavity?

The abdominal cavity is contained in an enclosure formed by:

• bony structures (the lower circumference of the ribs, the lumbar spine, and the pelvis)

• muscles (the diaphragm on top, the abdominal muscles on the sides, and the pelvic floor at the bottom).

The bony structures are somewhat *deformable* at the top (ribs, spine) and *rigid* at the bottom (pelvis).

The muscular structures are, like other muscles, *contractile* and *elastic.*

128

Diaphragm and pulmonary elasticity

When the diaphragm contracts, it tends to pull the lungs toward the pelvis ("to the bottom" when standing).

Conversely, when the diaphragm relaxes, the lungs rise toward the top of the thorax and tend to pull on the diaphragm.

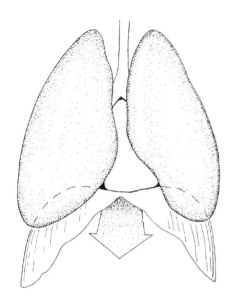 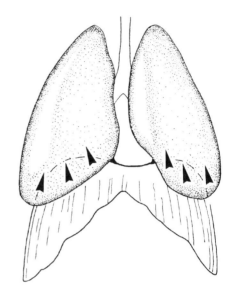

These two forces therefore always act *in opposite directions.*

People often think (erroneously) of this in reverse: that "the lungs press down on the diaphragm" or that "the diaphragm pushes the lungs upward while rising."

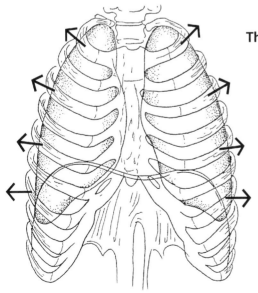

Thoracic cage and pulmonary elasticity

When the thoracic cage is opened, the lungs are stretched and expand (toward the sides, and from front to back).

Conversely, when the thoracic cage is not held in this open position, the elasticity of the lungs causes them to return to their original shape, which causes them to close (that is, the diameter decreases).

RESPIRATORY STOPS

During inhalation and exhalation, breathing manifests as airflow. Between these movements, there is a moment when breathing stops (normally for physiological reasons). These moments are called post-inspiratory apnea or post-expiratory apnea. *You can also stop the flow of air, voluntarily or involuntarily, using respiratory brakes or stops.*

Occlusives

Some of these stops create an occlusion, that is, a *closure* of the air passage, a little bit like turning off a faucet. These are called *occlusives.*

Examples:

- The glottis can close by bringing the vocal cords close together (glottal stop).
- The back of the tongue can flatten against the pharynx.
- You can simultaneously close the mouth and the nose (by pinching the nose).

In all these cases, *the airflow is totally stopped, at both inhalation and exhalation.*

Partial occlusives

You can also create an occlusion that only partially stops the airflow:

- The glottis can be partially closed and allow just a little bit of air through.
- The lips or the back of the tongue can be partially closed.

The occlusion can also occur in fits and starts, faster or slower, which will create a vibratory rhythm.

Examples:

- You can blow air through the mouth by vibrating the lips, like a horse snorting.
- You can make the soft palate vibrate above the tongue: this happens when you snore, during an inhalation.
- You can produce a vibration like a purr from the larynx.
- You can produce a sound by rapidly vibrating the vocal cords. (The voice itself is a type of partial occlusive.)

Occlusives can sometimes accumulate. Some types of pathology also produce occlusives, but are not discussed in this book.

An occlusive reduces the flow of air and prolongs the duration of an exhalation or inhalation. This can be significant, for example, when you want to *explore a specific respiratory volume more slowly or for a longer period.*

This can also allow the *inspiratory muscles to relax* during an exhalation in IRV when these muscles are working hard.

Occlusives allow you to play with high and low pressure between the two cavities (see "Techniques for decompressing the abdominal organs" on page 150).

SUSPENDED BREATHS

You can also voluntarily interrupt the airflow without producing an occlusion.

For example, inhale deeply and then exhale with an open mouth, nose, and glottis, and without creating vibrations during airflow. Now, while your airways are open, stop, as if in suspense, without blocking the breathing exits.

You have thus created an apnea *without closing the airways.* How can you achieve an apnea this way? By using *the forces that keep the lungs open* in order to prevent them from elastically returning to their original shape. During exhalation, these "opening" forces are the contractions of the muscles that keep the lungs stretched: the inspiratory muscles.

These methods of stopping airflow while "holding" the respiratory movement are called suspended breaths.

Thus, you can suspend exhalation while keeping the ribs open, or while keeping the diaphragm lowered, or by a combination of the two forces.

You can experiment with the same stops during inhalation.

Example: Inhale and then interrupt the inhalation in the same two ways described above.

Here, the force that stops the airflow comes from the inspiratory muscles, which stay statically contracted, suspending the inspiratory action.

These stops are involved when measuring out the air pressure under the vocal cords, which is practiced in some singing techniques (see page 157).

....

CHAPTER EIGHT

Analysis of the Principal Types of Breathing

DIAPHRAGMATIC BREATHING AND ITS VARIATIONS

This type of breathing is often called stomach breathing or abdominal breathing and especially affects the *inhalation phase.*

(The role of the diaphragm in exhalation is explored on page 140.)

Diaphragmatic breathing is most often practiced while at rest, breathing normally.

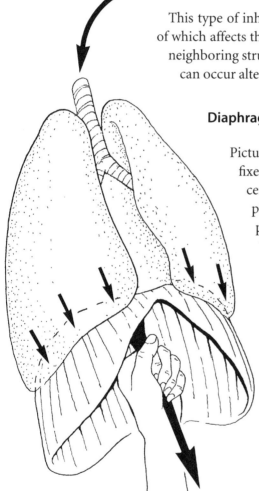

How does diaphragmatic inhalation work?

This type of inhalation utilizes two principal mechanisms, each of which affects the contraction of the diaphragm in relation to its neighboring structures in different ways. These two mechanisms can occur alternately or in succession.

Diaphragmatic inhalation: 1ˢᵀ mechanism

Picture the attachments of the diaphragm as being fixed on the circumference of the ribs, while the central tendon is mobile. Contraction of the diaphragm will pull the central tendon toward the pelvis. (When a person is standing, you can say "toward the floor;" you can then also say that the diaphragm is "lowered.")

At the top, this descent has an effect, via the pleura, on the bases of the lungs, which "elongate" toward the bottom.

This creates a negative pressure between the two, a "depression."

Thus a *vacuum* is created inside the lungs, which causes *inhalation.*

Below, the descent of the diaphragm pushes on the abdominal "water balloon" and deforms it. The area where this is most evident and where deformation is easiest is the front of the abdomen, where there is no bony structure to hinder movement. That is why the most common diaphragmatic breathing is often called "breathing through the abdomen."

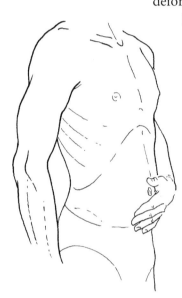

In the following pages we will see that the abdominal "water balloon" can be deformed in many other ways.

Important: The descent of the diaphragm is not simply a *fall,* which would require no effort and which would happen to any falling object through the forces of gravity. Gravity is the only factor coming into play when the abdomen moves down freely without muscle involvement.

In fact, however, the descent of the diaphragm encounters obstacles:

- the elastic resistance of the lungs

- the potential resistance of the abdomen. The abdomen resists forceful deformation, for example, when you wear tight clothing or a belt or girdle, or when the abdominal muscles are contracted and oppose any movement in the abdomen, or even in the case of obesity.

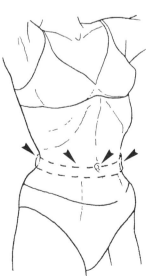

That is why the lowering of the central tendon is not always possible, or why it encounters limitations. In that case, there is a different type of diaphragmatic breathing (see page 138).

Variations on the first mechanism of diaphragmatic breathing

When the diaphragm pushes down, the abdominal cavity can respond in various ways. When the muscles in one part of the abdomen remain contracted, the abdominal "water balloon" cannot be deformed in that area. The deformation or bulging must occur somewhere else. That is why there can be a number of different versions of diaphragmatic breathing. Here we will describe variations on the most common type of inhalation described on the preceding page.

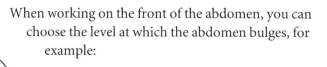

When working on the front of the abdomen, you can choose the level at which the abdomen bulges, for example:

• by breathing into only the lowest part of the abdomen (the area above the pubic bone), in which case the upper abdominal muscles are kept in contraction

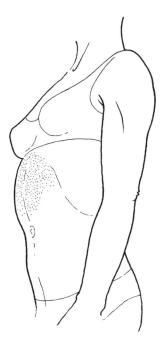

• by breathing into only the highest part of the abdomen (the epigastric area), in which case the lower abdominal muscles are kept in contraction

• by breathing into the abdomen only at the level of the waist, where only the abdominal muscles at that level are relaxed, while the muscles above and below are in contraction.

It is possible to contract the abdominal muscles at different levels because they are enervated by motor nerves from different levels of the medulla.

In the same way, you can produce an *asymmetric deformation* of the "water balloon." For example, you can round the abdomen only on the right or on the left. This is possible if you keep the abdominal muscles on the opposite side in contraction. Of course, you can also do *asymmetric breathing* at different levels.

Instead of deforming the front of the abdomen, you can *deform only the back* by moving the "water balloon" posteriorly. This gives you the sensation of rounding the back.

To do this, you must keep the anterior abdominal muscles contracted (especially the rectus abdominis). This is called *posterior diaphragmatic breathing*.

Here, too, posterior inhalation can be done at different levels and in an asymmetrical fashion.

You can prevent the deformation of the "water balloon" everywhere on the abdominal circumference, at the front, back, and sides. When this is done, the only area where the push of the diaphragm will cause movement is in the perineum. This is called *diaphragmatic perineal breathing*.

As you can see, diaphragmatic breathing using the first mechanism can take many forms and combinations.

What are the advantages of this type of diaphragmatic breathing?

- It is the most efficient way of performing maximum ventilation with a minimum of muscular effort.

- It mobilizes the abdominal organs, helps with their circulatory drainage, and sometimes even with their function (e.g., it is effective in treating constipation). This mobilization can affect all the organs, or it can be targeted more at one organ, by breathing precisely into that part of the abdomen where the targeted organ is located.

- The upper part of the trunk, that is, the rib and shoulder area, stays relaxed.

What are the disadvantages of this type of breathing?

The disadvantages occur when this type of breathing is done exclusively.

- It especially ventilates the base of the lungs, but not — or only very slightly — the top of the lungs.

- By pushing the abdominal mass toward the pelvis, it can contribute to a general descent of the organs, especially in the region of the lesser pelvis.

- It does not mobilize the rib cage very much. This can cause the rib cage to become rigid, and tend to stay in an expiratory position.

Exercises for practicing this type of diaphragmatic breathing can be found on pages 176 through 186.

Diaphragmatic inhalation: 2ND mechanism

When the central tendon of the diaphragm is immobilized, it forms a fixed point while the circumference is mobile. A contraction of the diaphragm pulls the lower ribs slightly upward toward the central tendon. Here, the diaphragm acts by *lifting the ribs*.

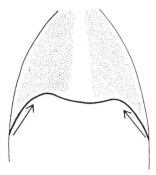

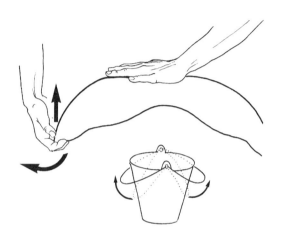

Remember that elevation of the ribs causes them to move apart laterally because of their shape as a bucket handle (see page 49). Here, the muscle acts as "lifter-separator" of the ribs because of their shape.

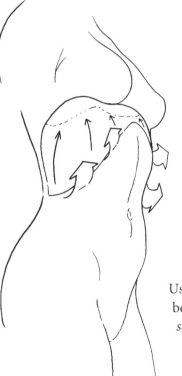

There is also another effect at work: At some point, the lowering of the central tendon reaches its maximum; because the abdominal mass does not allow for more upward deformation, it is then deformed laterally.

Using this second technique of diaphragmatic breathing, the belly does not bulge, but *the lower contour of the ribs lifts and separates at the same time.*

This respiratory movement also has many variations. For example, you can inhale by opening the lower ribs in the front or back, and you can also do it asymmetrically to the right or left only.

Most often, mechanisms 1 and 2 are mixed. In normal diaphragmatic breathing, the abdomen is lifted slightly and at the same time the ribs are moved slightly apart.

You can observe this when you watch a baby breathe while sleeping.

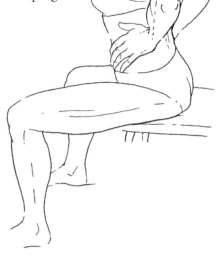

What are the advantages of diaphragmatic breathing with the second mechanism?

- It mobilizes the trunk in a region that is often tense due to stress, that is, in the upper part of the abdomen.

- It does not push the abdominal mass downward as forcefully as does the first mechanism.

What are the disadvantages of this type of breathing?

Since breathing is a mixture of costal and abdominal inhalation, these two types of inhalation are not as easy to distinguish from each other.

Exercises for practicing this type of diaphragmatic breathing can be found on pages 187 and 188.

The diaphragm and exhalation

Contrary to what you might think, the diaphragm does not cause exhalation because of its domed shape, which rises when you exhale. This is never due to the action of the diaphragm itself, but to other causes, which vary depending on the respiratory volume.

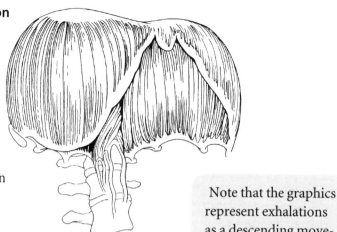

Note that the graphics represent exhalations as a descending movement, even though the diaphragm ascends during an exhalation.

However, the diaphragm may produce an action at the time of its rising, an action which often varies depending on the volume.

When exhaling tidal volume, pulmonary elasticity (see page 119) causes expiration and makes the diaphragm rise. The diaphragm may stay contracted in order to moderate or modulate the elastic recoil. This contraction is not very intense, however, and may be almost nonexistent.

On the other hand, *when exhaling after a large inhalation (IRV),* the force of the elastic recoil of the lungs is much stronger. Likewise, the contraction of the diaphragm is much stronger, especially if the IRV is very large. The contraction is strongest at the beginning of the exhalation, where the force of elastic recoil is at its maximum (see page 121).

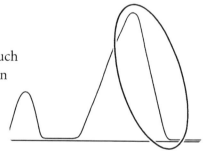

Note: The contraction of the diaphragm never *causes* exhalation to occur. Rather, it acts as a brake which is *opposed* to the movement and in proportion to its intensity.

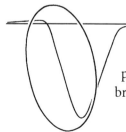

When exhaling ERV, the volume of the lungs diminishes due to the action of the expiratory muscles. Elastic recoil is no longer present. The diaphragm is no longer active, either as a participant or as a brake. It rises to its maximum position. This is a passive rising action.

COSTAL BREATHING AND ITS VARIATIONS

The mechanism of costal inhalation

During costal inhalation, the *diameter of the thoracic cage increases,* which causes the lungs to open. On page 39, we saw that elevating the ribs causes the diameter to increase, and that this elevation can be performed in the following ways:

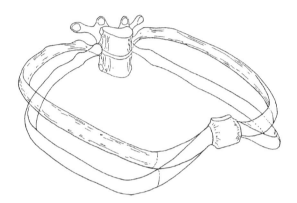

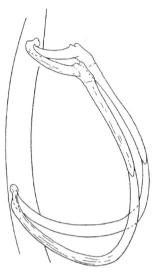

- more on the right or left for lateral elevation, similar to a bucket handle

- more from front to back elevating the sternum at the front, similar to the movement of an old-fashioned pump handle.

Thus, overall there are two primary directions for costal inhalation: (1) to the sides, and (2) from front to back.

All the muscles that are attached to the ribs and whose fibers run upward can participate in the action of costal inhalation. Each muscle works more in one direction than in the other, as we will see on the following pages.

Variations on costal inhalation

Within each of the two primary directions, the movements of costal inhalation show a lot of variation. For example, they can:

- mix and match
- accumulate in an inhalation of a very large IRV
- alternate during the course of one inhalation (e.g., an inhalation can move from lateral breathing from the lower ribs to breathing more into the top front)
- become asymmetrical
- involve precisely three or four ribs.

While diaphragmatic breathing varies due to a combination of interactions between the diaphragm and its environment, costal breathing varies for an entirely different reason: *the number of distinct costal inspiratory muscles, which individually move the rib cage in a very specific manner.*

On pages 87 through 105, we have seen that:

• The scalenes pull ribs 2 and 3 toward the sides.

• The SCM pulls the sternum upward and toward the front.

• The serratus anterior pulls ribs 7 through 10 upward and toward the sides.

• The pectoralis minor pulls ribs 3 through 5 upward and toward the front.

• The pectoralis major pulls ribs 6 through 8 upward and toward the sides.

- The back muscles extend the spine and lift the rib cage toward the front.

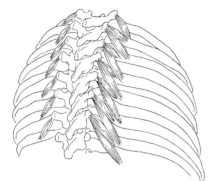

All of these muscles mobilize the rib cage in a variety of ways. This creates many variations in the types of costal inhalation.

What are the advantages of costal inhalation?

- It strengthens the costal muscles, especially around the circumference of the rib cage.

- It helps to keep the rib cage open, which is very important for those with a sedentary life style.

- By combining it with diaphragmatic breathing, it allows you to enlarge your inspiratory volume.

- It often goes hand in hand with an increase in muscle tone, and thus can be very energizing.

- The levatores costarum muscles pull the ribs upward and back, and the serratus posterior superior muscles pull ribs 1 through 4 upward and back.

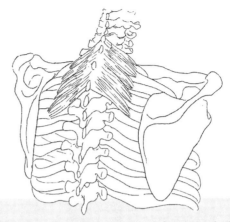

What are the disadvantages of costal inhalation?

- It is less efficient from a respiratory standpoint, because it requires greater muscular effort for a smaller air intake.

- If this is a person's primary way of breathing, when he or she elects to breathe consciously, this type of breathing can be very limiting and can prevent the person from finding and practicing diaphragmatic breathing.

- It can lead to overly strong contractions and rigidity in the thoracic area.

- It leads to a strong increase in muscle tone and can thus contribute to tension and stress.

- It can dominate the muscular effort in the upper thorax, which can lead to a "disconnect" between the lower and uppers parts of the trunk with respect to both the act of breathing and general body movement, which occur simultaneously. (This is especially true in voice training, where costal breathing occurs very close to the head and neck and where the muscular effort is concentrated in the same area.)

Exercises for practicing costal inhalation can be found on pages 189 through 199.

PARADOXICAL BREATHING

In this type of costal breathing the ribs open to such an extent that the lungs, elongated by an overly-stretched rib cage, raise the base of the lungs and the diaphragm too. The diaphragm then pulls the abdominal mass along with it.

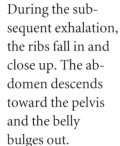

The result is that the belly moves strongly inward during inhalation, while the ribs expand.

During the subsequent exhalation, the ribs fall in and close up. The abdomen descends toward the pelvis and the belly bulges out.

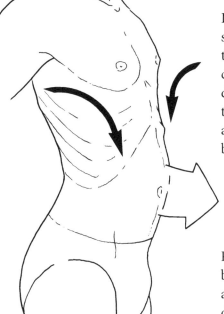

Paradoxical breathing is the opposite of diaphragmatic breathing. This is often the first type of breathing that a beginner discovers when trying to breathe with the diaphragm. Why? Because it uses the inspiratory costal muscles, which are very superficial and therefore easy to feel under the skin, while the contraction of the diaphragm, as we have seen on page 86, is not so easy to feel.

Beginners who want to see the effects of their breathing have a tendency to look first for respiratory movements in the thoracic area.

This is why learning to use diaphragmatic breathing must often be preceded by a "de-programming."

One way to "de-program" a person who is in the habit of doing paradoxical breathing is to have him or her start working on abdominal exhalation techniques. This will immediately improve the mobility of the abdomen during the next inhalation (see practice page 178).

What are the advantages of this type of breathing?

- It strengthens the costal inspiratory muscles. This may be important when these muscles need to be tonified, especially if the thoracic spine has a tendency to bend over slightly, or if the ribs are usually in a position that is too closed.

- It mobilizes the organs of the two cavities (see page 126) in a way that is opposite to that in which they are mobilized during diaphragmatic breathing.
    For this reason, it is a useful breathing technique to practice, alternating with diaphragmatic breathing, especially in the following cases:
    — In situations where intense diaphragmatic breathing is practiced (e.g., in voice training for speaking or singing) this type of breathing helps bring the system back into balance.
    — Every time you try to work with breathing to mobilize the internal organs (for relaxation, constipation, etc.). This type of breathing moves the organs in the opposite direction from that of the diaphragm.

- It creates a decompression of the abdominal organs (see page 150).

What are the disadvantages of this type of breathing?

- If this is the *only* type of breathing that a person does, paradoxical breathing can be very limiting because it prevents access to a variety of respiratory movements.

- If repeated too often, it brings about very strong contractions on the level of the thorax, which can make the area overly rigid.

- It can also lead to a tendency to guard the abdomen, which is always sucked in. Thus, it becomes very restrictive for the abdominal organs because it prevents their mobility.

For more information about paradoxical breathing, see page 180.

TWO MECHANISMS OF EXHALATION

Like inhalation, there are two very different mechanisms of exhalation:

- the thoracic mechanism, where you "close" the thoracic cage (opposite to how you would open it during costal inhalation)

- the abdominal mechanism, where you raise the abdomen (the "water balloon") toward the thoracic area. This compresses the lungs (opposite to how the same "water balloon" is lowered in diaphragmatic inhalation in order to expand the lungs).

Reminder: To exhale in tidal volume or IRV, it is not necessary to work the muscles because this type of exhalation is entirely due to the action of pulmonary elasticity.

1. Thoracic exhalation

There are two principal methods of "closing" the thoracic cage:

- You can make the ribs move closer to each other.
- You can drop the rib cage.

Both methods reduce the diameter of the thorax.

A. Moving the ribs closer together

This can be done by contracting the intercostal muscles. We have seen (page 104) that these muscles reduce the intercostal space.

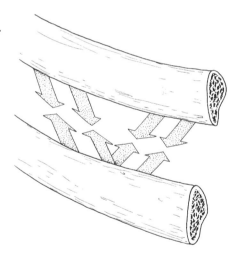

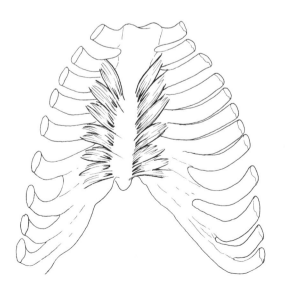

You can also bring the costal cartilages closer to each other and to the sternum. This is done with the transversus thoracis, which tightens the "fan" structure around the sternum so that it closes up.

B. Dropping the thoracic cage

This is the primary method for reducing the thoracic diameter.

Lowering of the rib cage occurs naturally due to the action of gravity in several positions: standing, lying on the back or on the stomach (see page 114).

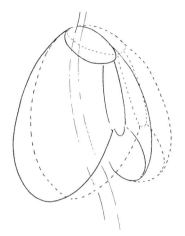

But it can also be caused by the muscles that pull the ribs toward the pelvis:

quadratus lumborum, latissimus dorsi, and serratus posterior inferior at the back,

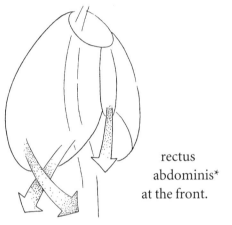

the internal and external obliques* on the sides,

rectus abdominis* at the front.

What are the advantages of costal exhalation?	*What are the disadvantages of this type of breathing?*

What are the advantages of costal exhalation?

- It moves the ribs and the costal cartilages in the direction of the expiratory movement.

- It is an important alternative action when a person has forcefully opened the ribs (especially in certain voice techniques).

What are the disadvantages of this type of breathing?

- When it is practiced almost exclusively, it contributes to a very weak and slender posture of the trunk, which can lead to an arched thoracic spine.

- It tends to first push the thorax, and then the abdomen, toward the pelvis (it can even cause the belly to bulge out) and may cause the organs of the lesser pelvis to prolapse.

....

* These muscles are more active in mobilizing the skeleton than in moving the abdominal "water balloon."

2. Abdominal exhalation

In this type of exhalation, the abdomen rises toward the thorax due to the muscles, which can push the abdominal "water balloon" upward and back. These are the abdominal muscles. This time, they do not move the ribs, but tighten up against the "water balloon."

A. Tightening the waist

The muscle that does the most "tightening" is the transversus abdominis. This muscle spreads almost all its contractile surface around the waist area.

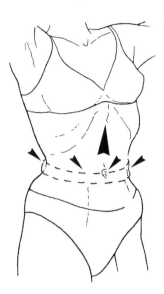

When it contracts, its horizontal fibers tighten up like a belt at the level of the umbilicus.

This pushes the upper half of the abdomen upward, which is an expiratory action.

At the same time, the other half of the abdomen is pushed downward.

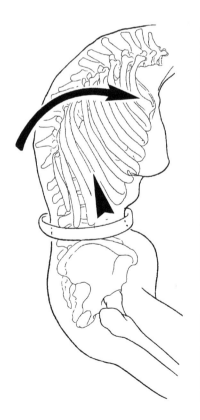

What are the advantages of this type of breathing?

- It is a very spontaneous movement, often associated with the flexion of the trunk, which is facilitated by gravity when the person is standing.
  This type of exhalation works well with the "sighing" action (see page 152). Thus, it can be included in any natural breathing training, especially when it is alternated with certain other, more refined, breathing techniques.

- It allows you to exhale without exerting too much pressure at the top of the trunk, keeping the circulation in the thorax loose.

What are the disadvantages of this type of breathing?

It presses on the organs at the bottom of the abdomen, which may cause the organs of the lesser pelvis to prolapse.

B. Raising the abdomen

You can also compress the abdominal "water balloon" from the bottom upwards. To do this, you must contract the muscles of the abdominal cavity, successively in an upward sequence.

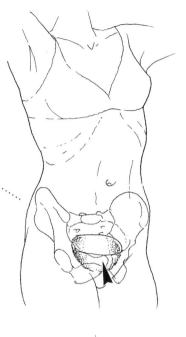

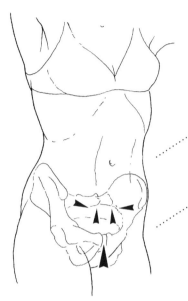

Starting from the bottom, first contract the muscles of the pelvic floor,

followed by the muscles at the lower anterior part of the abdomen,

without losing the contraction of the first muscles.

Continue successively contracting the abdominal muscles in an upward sequence while always keeping the lower muscles contracted.

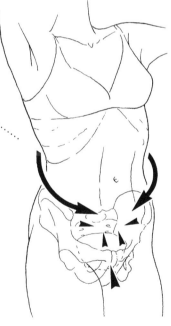

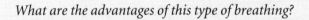

What are the advantages of this type of breathing?

- It strengthens the lower part of the trunk, providing a very protective support around the lumbar spine.

- It facilitates good coordination between the pelvic floor and the abdominal muscles.

What are the disadvantages of this type of breathing?

- It raises the abdominal mass, which can lead to vascular pressure in the thorax if the contraction is strong.

- It creates a framework of rising muscular synergy, which could lead to excessive muscle tension in the higher regions of the trunk and neck.

This represents a rising coordination of the pelvic floor/abdominal muscles.

TECHNIQUES FOR DECOMPRESSING THE ABDOMINAL ORGANS

The illustrations below show these techniques while lying down, but they can be performed in other positions as well.

Through the mutual interaction of the two cavities of the trunk, you can relieve the pressure from the abdominal "water balloon" which is usually exerted upon it. There are two techniques that help achieve this.

The first one consists of keeping the rib cage open while breathing out.

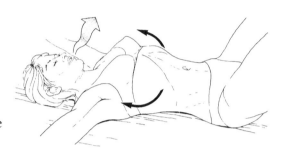

The lungs tend to operate with an elastic recoil during exhalation, but this is partially prevented by opening the ribs. Thus, the bases of the lungs rise, pulling the diaphragm and the abdominal organs along with them.

Another technique consists of initially exhaling a large amount of air and then closing the glottis (i.e., going into apnea at the end of the exhalation). At this point, you expand the rib cage as though breathing in, but without actually taking in air. This is sometimes called "mimicking an inhalation with closed glottis" or "making a false inhalation."

This stretches the lungs without refilling them with air. Instead of drawing air from the outside (see page 135), it draws the abdominal mass upward to the thorax.

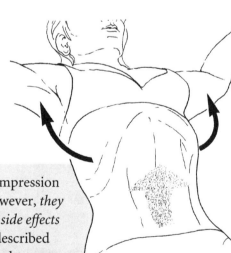

These two techniques are used especially in decompression movements for the organs of the lesser pelvis. However, *they are very complex exercises which have undesirable side effects if they are not done correctly.* They will therefore described at greater length in a future supplement. They are also mentioned on pages 135-137 of *The Female Pelvis* by this author.

VALSALVA'S METHOD

This is a technique that is especially designed for positioning the trunk. It mainly utilizes breathing to protect the spine (especially the lumbar spine) during risky situations that overstress it:

- while bending the spine, especially forward, to a high degree
- while carrying large loads in the arms or on the back
- while pushing, pulling, or raising something with great force.

Mechanism:

The principle underlying this method is to create a pocket in front of the spine like a rigid sack, which resists flexion, so that the vertebrae can solidly lean on it.

This reduces the tendency of the vertebrae to glide forward, and thus the need for the muscles of the back to prevent this gliding.

How it is performed:

Start by inhaling and lowering the diaphragm. Then close the glottis (i.e., stop breathing) and keep the diaphragm in its lowered position. Now contract the abdominal muscles around the entire circumference of the waist as well as the muscles of the pelvic floor. The abdominal mass is now safely contained on all sides and pressed against the spine.

What is the effect of Valsalva's method on structures other than the spine?

- Either the pressure exerted on the abdomen is reflected downward (one can feel a very strong push toward the perineum, which is hard to resist if the perineal muscles are weak); or

- The pressure exerted on the abdomen is reflected upward (which slows down thoracic circulation).

In addition, you can feel a strong pressure toward the neck and the head, which can lead to congestion of the blood vessels.

These consequences can be harmful if the maneuver is performed with too much force or by those who are not strong enough.

THE SIGH: RELAXING THE DIAPHRAGM

This is a small exhalation which you can do spontaneously to relax.

The difference between this and a normal exhalation is that the sigh has a slight momentum, an acceleration in the airflow. This momentum can accelerate the beginning or the end of the sigh, depending on the situation.

The sigh occurs most often during an exhalation of tidal volume. So it is the elastic recoil force of the lungs that is involved in this exhalation, rather than the expiratory muscles. In addition, the ribs drop and the thoracic spine is slightly flexed, because the posture muscles usually relax during a sigh.

Pulmonary elasticity is truly "released" and the inspiratory muscles do not make even a minimal attempt to prevent it from rebounding. This is what creates the acceleration in the airflow.

The sigh can be accompanied by a small "support movement," a moment where the air is slowed down via a slight occlusive before the lungs are released completely. There may be a small additional sound from the vocal cords, without producing a specific vowel in the mouth. There may also be a breathing sound if you try to keep the lips shut.

During this short moment, which lasts the time of an exhalation in tidal volume, the muscles are visibly relaxed. The apnea, which usually follows a sigh, is longer, as if to deepen this state (see the following page).

For a brief moment, the sigh is both evidence of, and a means of, relaxation for a large part of the postural and respiratory musculature, especially the diaphragm.

It is especially suitable for movements which occur during rest or relaxation, and for fluid or smooth movements.

In addition, when accompanied by a slight sound, it can be used in voice techniques when a person tries to recover relaxation or vocal spontaneity.

Post-expiratory pause: the apnea following an exhalation of tidal volume

At some point during exhalation following a time of normal, relaxed breathing, the respiratory system reaches a state of equilibrium between:

- the pulmonary elastic recoil force, which has caused the lungs to return to their original shape

- relaxation of the inspiratory muscles (i.e., the muscles are no longer contracted).

In physics, equilibrium is described as a "state of rest between forces that cancel each other out." Thus, this is a state of rest between physiological forces.

The moment which follows an exhalation of tidal volume and that precedes the next inhalation is a time of apnea (without respiratory movement). This apnea is not due to an obstruction or an active movement. *It is a time when all the structures relax.* Consequently, it is a time when the general body tension relaxes as well. We call it "a moment of post-expiratory pause."

What are the benefits of such a moment?

- This moment is essential for relaxation techniques. You can also try to reproduce this moment in times of stress, or to prepare for such times.

- It usually occurs during sleep, but you can also use it to help you fall asleep.

- You can use it in daily life to experience a "mini-relaxation."

Exercises for achieving this restful moment can be found on page 205.

Hiccupping

A hiccup occurs when there is a sudden involuntary contraction of the diaphragm and an identical contraction of the costal inspiratory muscles. This forcefully opens the thorax and would cause a quick inhalation were it not for an immediate and simultaneous closing of the glottis.

This inspiratory action suddenly stretches the pulmonary tissue. However, since the glottis is closed and the lungs cannot be filled with air, the thorax suddenly sucks the abdomen toward it. Especially in babies, you can see how the epigastric region is suddenly depressed during a hiccup.

Coughing

Coughing is an action which is usually intended to eject something from the respiratory tract. To achieve this, air is abruptly and very quickly released from the lungs.

Here is a detailed description of what happens during a cough:

• First, the glottis is closed (the vocal cords are dynamically moved closer to each other) and compressed air accumulates under the closed glottis. The expiratory muscles (abdominals, perineal muscles, and costal expiratory muscles) compress the lungs, as if to prepare for a large ERV, but with a closed glottis.

• Then the glottis is suddenly opened and the air under pressure escapes all at once.

The cough can be used to eject an object or phlegm, which is trapped in the lungs or bronchi. But it can also occur when there is nothing to eject, for instance, as a reaction to an irritation of the bronchial mucosa. This is a dry cough.

In either case, the cough is a mechanism that involves both the abdominal and thoracic cavities and which exerts a very strong counter-pressure toward the perineum. It is therefore important that the perineum have sufficient muscle tone to withstand the pressure.

Sneezing

The sneeze is a very strong and almost irrepressible cough, which happens due to an irritation (often from an allergy) of the nasal mucosa. The mechanism is the same as with the cough, but much faster and more intense. Also, in a sneeze, part of the expelled air exits through the nose.

Voice production

The voice is produced during an expiratory action (expiration of tidal volume, IRV or ERV). The exhaled air starts vibrating at the level of the vocal cords. This produces the first sound, which is then filtered and enriched by the resonators and articulation structures of the throat.

Crying

During crying we can find the same elements as during voice production. There is only one difference: The air pressure during crying is much stronger due to the fact that a large airflow is created by the expiratory muscles, and, at the same time, the vocal cords are dynamically narrowed and tightened. The power of the sound is related to the rate of the airflow. Spontaneous crying is often linked to a type of exhalation from the top of the abdomen (described on page 148).

Panting

When panting, one increases the frequency of breaths with small volumes. At the same time, apneas are eliminated, especially post-expiratory apneas.

Panting can accentuate inhalation, as when you try to "catch your breath" very quickly. This mode of breathing readily leads to hyperventilation because the frequency of breathing is increased while apneas are either shortened or suppressed altogether. It often occurs during sexual intercourse. It is sometimes used in breathing techniques which aim at working with and resolving emotions (e.g., psychotherapies and somatotherapies).

Panting can also accentuate exhalation. It is sometimes used to practice successive sighing, for example, to help a person deal with pain. It can also be a method associated with very strong fatigue, because the air intake is mainly passive. This allows the body to relieve the work of the inspiratory muscles, especially the diaphragm (see also page 215).

Laughing

During laughing the air exits under pressure, with a vocal sound (i.e., the vocal cords are vibrating). In addition, the air and voice output is interrupted rapidly and rhythmically.

Like coughing, laughing involves a certain acceleration of airflow and pressure (though less than during a cough). Each time the glottis is closed, a brief sound is formed under air pressure. This pressure is created by the contraction of expiratory muscles, especially of the abdominal muscles, which explains why laughing a lot can cause a belly ache.

Thrusting push downward

During this movement there is a simultaneous contraction of the diaphragm, which pushes the abdominal mass toward the perineum, and the abdominal muscles, which push on the circumference of the trunk. At the same time, the perineum releases one of its sphincters, the urethra for urination or the anus for defecation, and, for a woman, the vagina during the birthing process. The thrusting force is very strong (often too strong) for the perineum. It is often better to moderate or even avoid them whenever possible.

Breathing during sleep

During sleep the body uses the most economical type of breathing with respect to the muscles. Sleeping on your side is the most efficient type of breathing: the abdominal mass falls forward toward the surface of the bed. This brings the diaphragm into inspiratory position, which enables it to work minimally at each inhalation.

During exhalation, the lungs rise and pull along the diaphragm, which returns to a slightly higher position. This is an exhalation of tidal volume, without muscle action.

Exhalation with bulging belly

As we have seen on page 144, during paradoxical breathing, the abdomen is pulled upward toward the thorax during inhalation. During exhalation, it drops downward and forward.

It is also possible to exhale by intentionally *pushing* the abdomen downward. To do this, you must simultaneously lower the ribs (see page 147) and push down the belly by contracting the diaphragm.

This type of exhalation sometimes accompanies lower expulsive movements (defecation, urination). It is also used in some sitting meditation postures. Last but not least, it can be used in voice training to strongly moderate the recoil force of the lungs during passages that require a high proportion of the airflow.

Inspiratory actions during expiration

As previously noted (page 15), breathing and respiration are not always the same thing.

Usually, you inhale by performing an inspiratory action, by opening the thoracic cage and/or by lowering the diaphragm. Then you exhale by letting these structures return to their expiratory position, that is, the thoracic cage is lowered and/or the diaphragm rises.

But it is also possible to keep or even drag this structure into an inspiratory position during exhalation:

You can keep the diaphragm lowered during exhalation.

You can also keep the ribs open. You can even open them further while breathing out.

In this case, the inspiratory muscles continue to contract during exhalation. They even work extremely hard, since they oppose the elastic recoil force of the lungs: The diaphragm slows the rising of the base of the lungs, and the costal inspiratory muscles slow down the retreat of the lungs under the ribs.

This breathing practice can produce very different results:

- It can help to mobilize the abdominal mass.

- It can suspend the breath during exhalation, allowing you to measure out the air-flow. This is often used as a warm-up technique in preparing for singing or playing a wind instrument. (This will be further explored in a later supplement to this book.)

SECTION 2

CHAPTER NINE

....

Practice Pages

THE PURPOSE OF these pages is not to demonstrate a particular method of breathing, nor to present a complete repertoire of breathing methods. Rather, the idea is to help you experiment with a number of things that were illustrated in the first part of the book, and to provide a foundation in different movements that can be combined in a variety of ways.

Important warning: These practice pages present a variety of exercises, including the exploration of specific sensations, the actions of specific muscles, and the combination of muscle actions during specific respiratory movements.

These exercises are not offered for therapeutic purposes, but rather as ideas for increasing awareness of the body and for sparking a new sense of living. *They do not make allowance for possible pathologies.*

In the event that they are intended as part of a therapeutic program, the therapist must adapt them appropriately to the needs of certain pathologies.

Some of these exercises will not be appropriate under all circumstances. It is important to make the right choices and know the contraindications and precautions for those who have been injured or who are being treated for back pain, rheumatoid arthritis, organ disease, cardiovascular or respiratory disease, cancer, or for neurological or psychiatric disorders. In all of these situations, it is important to *consult your physician.*

On the following pages, you will find exercises for:

- Preparing the body for breathing exercises (pages 161–175)
- Experimenting with diaphragmatic inhalation (pages 176–188)
- Experimenting with costal inhalation (pages 189–199)
- Experimenting with costal exhalation (pages 200–201)
- Experimenting with abdominal exhalation (pages 202–203)
- Experimenting with different respiratory volumes (pages 204–209)
- Combining several respiratory movements (pages 210–215)

PREPARING FOR BREATHING EXERCISES

The following pages present exercises that will help prepare certain parts of the body for breathing exercises. They are not breathing exercises themselves.

What these exercises have in common is that they prepare the thoracic cage for various breathing movements.

Subtly and imperceptibly to most of us, the thoracic region becomes more rigid over time. Good mobility of the rib cage is important, however, because it allows us to explore an unexpected range of breathing movements. More importantly, it permits a much better quality of movement, more suppleness, fluidity, and ease in combining movements.

Important: Making the thoracic cage more supple does not only mean to open it more. In fact, mobility can be explored and increased through focusing on both opening *and* closing.

The following exercises are especially recommended for people who need greater amplitude of breath, both for inhalation and exhalation. This would include, for example, professional speakers or singers, musicians who play wind instruments, and those engaged in sports (especially swimmers and divers).

They are also suitable for people who have breathing difficulties, for example, due to asthma or chronic bronchitis. However, in these cases, it is imperative to work with a physical therapist, at least at the beginning. The therapist can help tailor the exercises to the individual.

There are several preparatory exercises:

1. Some are designed more for exercising the flexibility of the ribs themselves and their capacity to modify the curvature of the rib cage (page 162).

2. Some help exercise the articulations between the ribs and the vertebrae (page 165).

3. Some are designed to stretch the intercostal muscles and to allow the ribs to move apart better (page 166).

4. Some help to make the big muscles of the thorax more supple. These are the muscles that link the thorax to the abdomen, head, and shoulders (page 168).

5. Some help to relax the epigastric area (page 172).

6. Some help to stretch the diaphragm (page 173).

1. Curving the ribs

Pushing the ribs with the hands

In standing position, put the palm of your right hand on the right side of your ribs. Feel how you can push at this point in particular and deform the curvature of the thorax.

Try the same action with a hand on both sides of the rib cage. Push the ribs on the right and left toward the center of the thorax. This will narrow the thorax.

Look for the same effect in the front, on each side of the costal angle. Press from front to back, or from right to left. This is the area where the longest and most flexible costal cartilages are located. Then feel for the ribs at the back just above the waist and press again. This may be a little more difficult.

Now try to press simultaneously backwards on one side and forward on the other to produce an asymmetrical shape of the costal "cylinder."

When you try to press the ribs on a higher level, they may seem more rigid. For these less mobile areas of the rib cage, the exercises on the following pages are more effective. The ribs there are moved more easily by pressing against a support to apply counter pressure.

You can use the backrest of a chair to help you push back the ribs in all different directions.

Placing an object under the ribs

For this, you need a soft object with the shape of a half-inflated ball. (A cushion may also be used.) Stretch out on the floor. Observe the contact and support points of your thorax on the floor.

Now place the soft object under your right ribs at mid-level, at about the lower margin of the shoulder blade and a little bit below. Place it 10cm (4 inches) away from the spine, so that it juts out from under your ribs.

Take the time to get into the right position, to feel the ribs and how they adapt to the uneven surface. Do they get pushed back, and how much do they resist?

Modifying the support under the ribs by moving the head

Slowly turn your head to the right or left. Make easy movements, without forcing it. The goal is not to turn your neck as far as possible, but to feel that, for example, as you turn your head to the right, you also move your right thorax (especially the top part) and bring your ribs more onto the cushion.

The ribs should get pushed back a little, curved a little more. Repeat this several times, and feel how you need to moderate the pressure of the cushion on the ribs. It is more important to vary the movement or increase/decrease the pressure during a repetition than to go further.

Modifying the support under the ribs by moving the hips

Bring the hips, knees, and ankles into flexion, with both feet flat on the floor. Lift the right foot while gently "unfolding" your knee.

With the foot pointing upward, trace little circles in the air. They should be no more than 20cm (8 inches) in diameter. This is enough to help you feel how the pelvis and ribs (especially the lower ribs) are supported differently on the cushion. Here again, the important thing is not to move the leg fast or to trace wide circles, but to do the circles in order to move the ribs.

Repeat this movement about 10 times.

Modifying the support of the ribs by moving the arms

With your two hands joined and fingers intertwined, place the arms above your chest pointing upward while gently tensing your elbows. Focus on how you can pull your shoulder blades away from the floor.

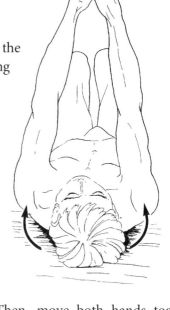

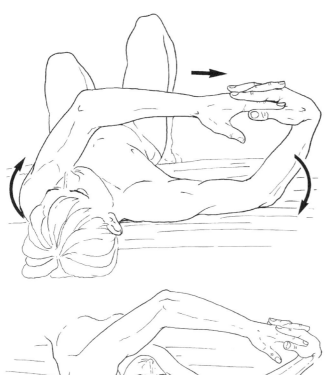

Then, move both hands together to the right and then to the left, alternately using the flexion of one of the elbows so that the flexed arm pulls the straightened arm.

As you become more flexible, try to pull and lift the opposite shoulder blade off the ground.

Notice again how the ribs (this time the middle ribs) are pushed back and deformed against the outline of the cushion as the pressure changes with the movement of the arm. Repeat this movement about 10 times.

When you finish this exercise, stretch as much as possible. Feel how the ribs touch the ground and how this feeling has changed since before the exercise. How is it on the right, on the left? How are you positioned? What does the structure that you lean on (cushion, floor) feel like? When you breathe into your ribs, how is it different on each side? Now start again, but this time begin with the other side. Then, get up and feel how your costal breathing has changed.

This whole exercise provides much greater mobility of the ribs, especially in the back, but also indirectly in the front. It allows you to address the costal breathing shown on pages 189–199 in a much more effective way.

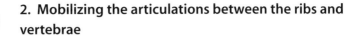

2. Mobilizing the articulations between the ribs and vertebrae

This time you have to look for movement in an area that is much closer to the spine. To mobilize this area, you need to have a thin object (about 50cm [20 inches] in length) which you can press against. This can be a soft object, such as a small rolled-up towel, or a hard object, such as a stick with a small diameter (no more than a few centimeters).

Again, stretch out on the ground and place the object on one side of the thoracic spine, about 6cm (2.5 inches) from the spinous processes.

The object should be just outside the transverse processes, at the spot where you feel the ribs start.

Now do the same movements described on the three preceding pages. The new object that you press against will affect the mobility in the joints between the ribs and vertebrae. The movement will be felt much more clearly at the middle of the back. In daily life, these barely move. When their capsules and ligaments are mobilized, you will become very aware of the sensations in the back and thorax at a specific area. As you become aware of this new mobility there, you will be able to perceive posterior costal breathing more clearly (see pages 196 and 197).

165

3. Stretching the muscles between the ribs

Bringing the rib cage into an asymmetrical position

For this exercise, use a larger object (the size of a big pillow) of medium hardness. Put it on the floor and lean sideways against it with your thorax, with the hips, knees, and ankles bent slightly in front of you. Feel how the object molds your thorax.

On the side facing the ceiling, your ribs will be pulled apart, somewhat like the ribs of a fan. On the side leaning against the object, on the other hand, the ribs will be closer together, almost touching each other.

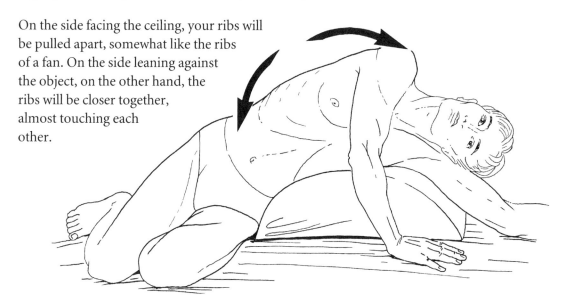

Opening the thoracic cage on the inside

Visualize the right half of your thorax as if it were open, as if you were inspecting a hollow space (an igloo or tent, for example). Now, in your mind, model this hollow space from the inside by making it bigger and opening the spaces between the ribs.

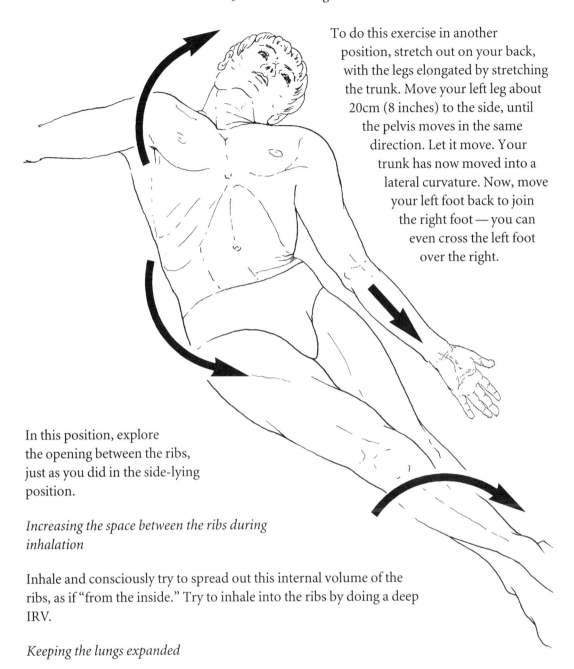

To do this exercise in another position, stretch out on your back, with the legs elongated by stretching the trunk. Move your left leg about 20cm (8 inches) to the side, until the pelvis moves in the same direction. Let it move. Your trunk has now moved into a lateral curvature. Now, move your left foot back to join the right foot — you can even cross the left foot over the right.

In this position, explore the opening between the ribs, just as you did in the side-lying position.

Increasing the space between the ribs during inhalation

Inhale and consciously try to spread out this internal volume of the ribs, as if "from the inside." Try to inhale into the ribs by doing a deep IRV.

Keeping the lungs expanded

When you've inhaled as much as you possibly can, stop breathing for several seconds (apnea) and remain in this inspiratory position. Feel how the rib cage stays open. The inspiratory muscles in this area work to keep the thorax open.

Narrowing the space between the ribs during exhalation

Take a few more normal breaths. Then, while you are exhaling, extend the exhalation into an ERV by "closing" your thoracic cage on the narrower side.

4. Stretching the big muscles which run toward the ribs

Do the same exercises on the preceding page, but add the arm to the posture.

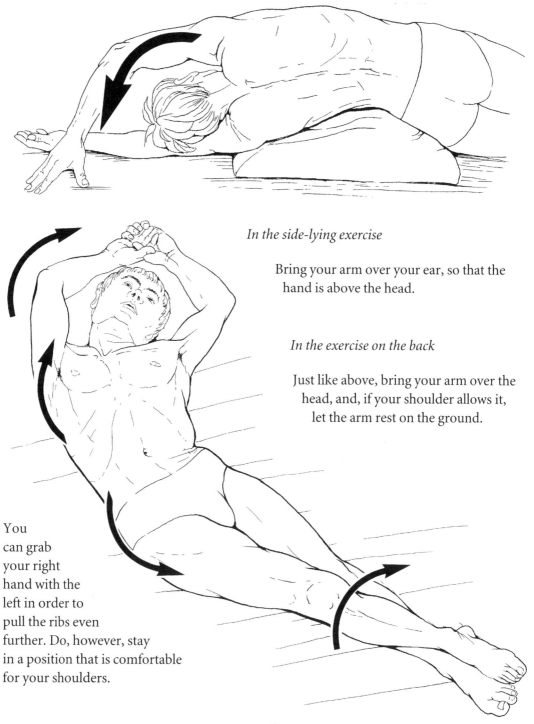

In the side-lying exercise

Bring your arm over your ear, so that the hand is above the head.

In the exercise on the back

Just like above, bring your arm over the head, and, if your shoulder allows it, let the arm rest on the ground.

You can grab your right hand with the left in order to pull the ribs even further. Do, however, stay in a position that is comfortable for your shoulders.

Feel how this opens up your ribs even more. You have just stretched three big muscles of the trunk: pectoralis major in the front, serratus anterior on the side, and latissimus dorsi on the back. These three muscles have pulled your thoracic cage.

Breathing into the "helping" side

In these two positions, you can use costal breathing to augment the effect of the movement. Start by breathing in the most obvious way: Inhale into the elongated side to open it even more. Try to keep this position for an apnea that lasts several seconds. Exhale into the narrower side to close it more and to accentuate the curvature.

Using exhalation to stretch

In this position, continue by exhaling in a large ERV. The muscles are stretched by the rebound position of the ribs.

Generally, you can reproduce the same elongation that these muscles would produce by moving the ribs and arms simultaneously in different positions.

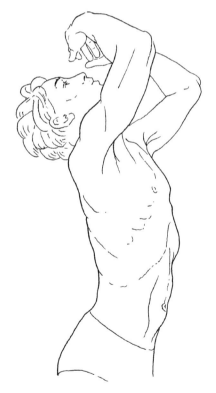 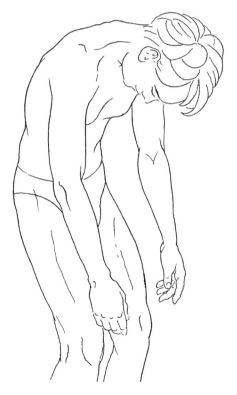

For example, you can bend your spine backwards to open the thoracic cage at the front, and you can extend the effect of this position by moving the arms forward and upward.

You can curve the thoracic spine forward to move the ribs on the back further apart, and you can accentuate this by bringing the arms toward the front of the trunk.

Stretching the pectoral muscles

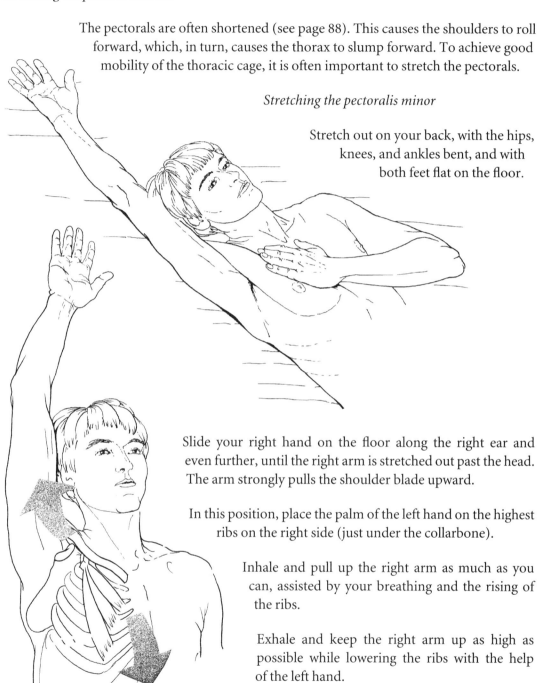

The pectorals are often shortened (see page 88). This causes the shoulders to roll forward, which, in turn, causes the thorax to slump forward. To achieve good mobility of the thoracic cage, it is often important to stretch the pectorals.

Stretching the pectoralis minor

Stretch out on your back, with the hips, knees, and ankles bent, and with both feet flat on the floor.

Slide your right hand on the floor along the right ear and even further, until the right arm is stretched out past the head. The arm strongly pulls the shoulder blade upward.

In this position, place the palm of the left hand on the highest ribs on the right side (just under the collarbone).

Inhale and pull up the right arm as much as you can, assisted by your breathing and the rising of the ribs.

Exhale and keep the right arm up as high as possible while lowering the ribs with the help of the left hand.

Do one or two easy breaths. Repeat this movement three to five times. Then, place both arms on the floor on each side of the body. Feel the shoulder blades and the arms touch the floor, and feel the movement of the thoracic cage. Now repeat this exercise on the other side.

Stretching the pectoralis major

Stretch out on your back. Pull up both bent knees toward the stomach and bring them to the left side of the trunk by twisting the waist.

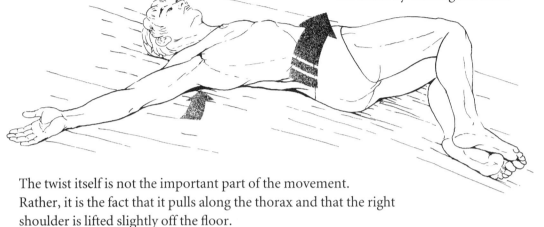

The twist itself is not the important part of the movement. Rather, it is the fact that it pulls along the thorax and that the right shoulder is lifted slightly off the floor.

Pay attention to how you can control the lifting of the shoulder by moving the knees: If they are lifted off the floor too much, the stretching effect may be too strong. If they are too close to the floor, the movement may have no effect.

From this position, move your right arm to the side while keeping the elbow on the floor. Slide your arm, making a large arc on the floor. With your shoulder lifted off the floor, your arm will be slightly behind the plane of the trunk.

While you do this exercise, you can feel how the pectoralis major is stretched at the front of the chest and at the anterior edge of the armpit.

Note: You have to moderate this stretching. Make sure it feels comfortable. If it is too strong, move the knees closer to the stomach to bring the right shoulder closer to the floor. Then rotate your right wrist inward and outward to pull the arm and shoulder in the same direction. You will feel different areas of the pectoralis major stretch out, depending on your movements.

Repeat these movements three to five times. Then, position both arms on either side of the body. As with the pectoralis minor, pay attention to the contact of the shoulder blade with the floor and the mobility of the left and right ribs. Then repeat this exercise on the other side.

5. Relaxing the lower rib cage and epigastric area

The epigastric area (under the xiphoid process of the sternum) is often tense. To prepare the body for diaphragmatic work, it is important to first relax this area.

Stretch out on your back in the same position as shown on page 163.

With your fingertips, palpate the edge of the rib cage, on the front part of your trunk. Run your fingers along the costal angle, which is formed by the xiphoid process of the sternum and the costal cartilages.

Gently "march" your fingers along this border so that you get to know it well. Then, try to squeeze a fold of skin in this area. Start where it is easiest. If it doesn't work, don't force it.

When you are able to squeeze a fold of skin, pull it gently away from the rib cage ("pinch an inch," no more). Do this during exhalation (an exhalation or sigh of tidal volume).

Try to use a "sigh" to relax this area. After releasing the skin fold, inhale/exhale/pause as if into this area. Repeat this maneuver every 5-10cm (2-4 inches). Then, check to see whether this changes your breathing. Next, put together your three middle fingers and place them just underneath the edge of the rib cage, where it seems easiest.

While inhaling, press down slightly with your fingers and do as if you were to inhale by pushing back your hand. This is a diaphragmatic inhalation, where the diaphragm pushes against the fingers.

While exhaling, let your fingers sink in slightly, without applying any pressure. (If it makes you feel uncomfortable, stop.) Now release your fingers.

You can complete the exercise in the same manner in the region of the abdomen at the top of the costal angle. This region corresponds to the area where the stomach, liver, and, slightly more to the back, the pancreas are located.

6. Stretching the diaphragm

The diaphragm can be stretched and elongated like any other muscle. And, like any muscle that you want to stretch, you must make it do the opposite of its usual action. Since it is an inspiratory muscle, *you must use exhalation to stretch it.* To really stretch it completely, you must do an exhalation that is as complete as possible, all the way to the end of an ERV. This makes the central tendon rise to its maximum height. Only at this extreme position is the diaphragm really stretched.

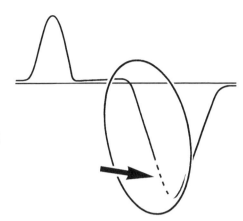

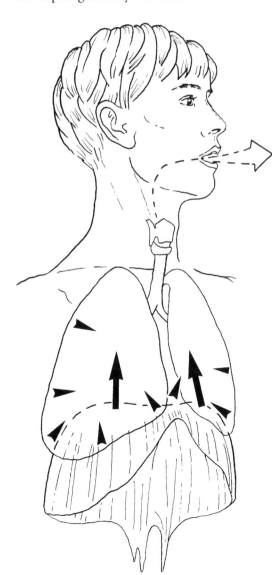

How can you be sure that you have reached maximum ERV? To be sure, you will never feel the absolute limit. A residual volume of air will always remain in your lungs, and you can never know for certain that you have reached the maximum possible exhalation.

This is why you will have to force an exhalation that lasts as long as you can possibly make it *while keeping the mouth and even the bottom of your throat completely open.* This will help achieve the maximum possible quantity of exhaled air very quickly.

On the other hand, you will find that the more the diaphragm is stretched, the greater the tendency to transform the big exhalation into a small thread of air by forming an occlusive (generally in the mouth): You start making the "*ffff*" or "*ssss*" sounds and pressing the lips together so that the air escapes more slowly. This prevents you from going into a very large amplitude of ERV and prevents the diaphragm from being fully stretched.

Make sure that you keep your glottis open during this exhalation, especially when you try to stretch the diaphragm with the postures on the following pages.

Using different postures to stretch the diaphragm

Sit on the floor. With your arms behind your back and elbows bent to support yourself, pull your back backwards and upwards to stretch it as much as you can.

Now, bend at your hips and pull the knees to your stomach to elongate the low back.

Then place one foot at a time on the floor, with your hips and knees bent, and try to stretch your back as much as possible.

Place your arms on the floor above your head and stretch as far as you can. The goal here is not to make the shoulders more flexible, but to move the ribs into an open position by elevating the arms. Inhale a large amount of air in IRV.

Use this inhalation to open the ribs even further, and pull your arms up even more. Now open your mouth and breathe out from the bottom of your throat while keeping the back of the neck on the floor.

Exhale as much as you possibly can, while keeping the arms stretched upward as far as possible and the ribs as open as possible.

To do this, breathe out with your mouth and glottis open, as shown on the previous page.

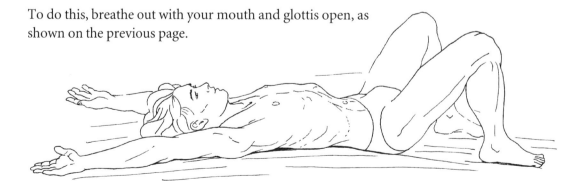

Pay attention to the following two points:

• Keep your neck stretched out and close to the floor — it will try to bend the more deeply you exhale.

To do this, you must hold a position with the chin slightly retracted during this exercise.

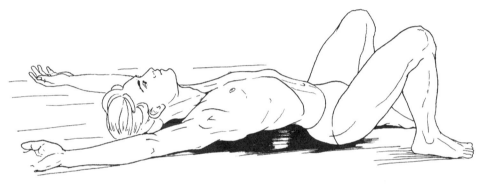

• Keep the lower back on the floor. The area around the waist will try to arch upward, too, the more you exhale. Why? Because the diaphragm, which is stretched around the ribs, compensates by pulling at the lumbar attachments, causing a lordosis of the back.

To do this, keep your knees flexed, or place yourself in a position with knees bent and pulled to your stomach. In fact, if you practice with stretched legs, the arch at the waist can become pretty large, and in that case, the diaphragm will not really be stretched.

A simple way to stretch the diaphragm is to use all the elements of the exercise while standing: arms lifted, deep exhalations.

DIAPHRAGMATIC INHALATIONS

The following pages describe practical exercises for many different types of breathing. What they have in common is that all are caused by the contraction of the diaphragm. Each exercise is presented separately, but they can be combined or used with costal breathing.

Diaphragmatic inhalation — 1st mechanism

In this first series of breathing exercises the diaphragm is lowered, pulling the central tendon toward the pelvis, while its lower insertions (around the ribs) do not move or move very little (see pages 134-137).

Exercise 1: Observing spontaneous breathing

All these exercises are described with the person lying on their back. This position avoids many postural contractions which would interfere with the sensations felt during the true breathing movements. Yet all these exercises can be practiced in other positions. In fact, once you are past the initial learning phase, it would be a good idea to reproduce these sensations in other positions.

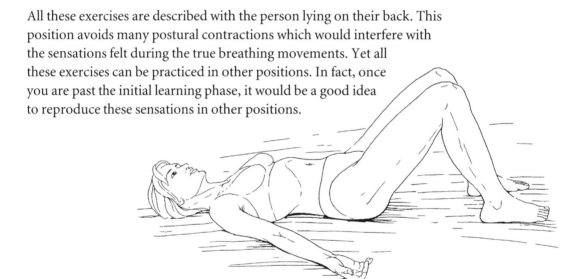

Position yourself on your back, on a comfortable surface of medium hardness (a foam mattress or the carpet). Flex your hips, knees, and ankles, and put your feet flat on the floor, with the back in an elongated position. The abdominal muscles are relaxed, the anterior movement of the abdomen unconstrained.

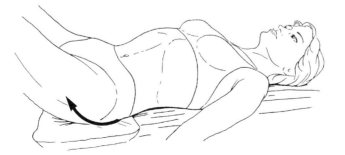

To start, you can even lift the pelvis into a retroverted position by placing a cushion under the coccyx and the base of the sacrum. This will loosen up abdominal movement even more.

Now, put one hand on the abdomen and the other on the sternum.

Relax as much as you can by "melting" into the floor. Use the contact points of your body to allow your weight to sink in as much as possible.

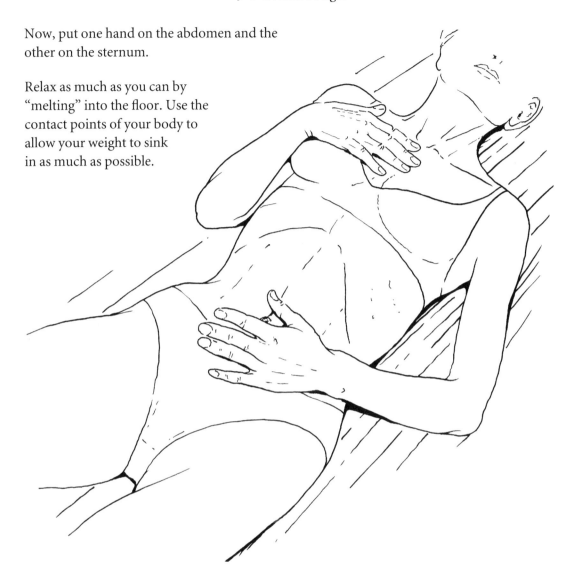

Start by observing where the respiratory movement takes place at the moment.

Try to recognize the area that moves, even if it is very small (your body does not need much air in this position). Can you feel this movement more under your hand on the stomach, or on the ribs?

Take your time to recognize what is happening without making assumptions about what you learned about good or bad breathing. Just observe. This is a more subtle action than it seems because usually, when you observe breathing, you also transform it.

It is very important to do this observation before starting the exercises on the following pages, where you *will* interfere with your breathing. It would also be a good idea to come back to this first observation regularly, between the series of breathing that follow.

Exercise 2: *Lengthening your exhalation*

Instead of simply observing your breathing, you will now interfere with it to shape it, making it into a specific type of breathing. This will no longer be a spontaneous movement.

As you breathe, pay attention to each expiratory movement. Each time you exhale, simply try to lengthen the exhalation very slightly, or make it slightly more intense.

Now, can you change the exhalation so that only the lower hand moves? While exhaling, your abdomen sinks inward slightly under your hand.

Once you have localized this movement, try to boost its amplitude. Exhale in ERV where you can strongly feel how the abdomen sinks inward. (However, do not try to reach the maximum possible ERV, which would also move the ribs. It is important to interfere only with your abdominal movement.)

Later, you can add a sound to the movement, for example, "*ffff*" or "*chhhhh.*" Try to prolong the sound without making it stronger. Pay attention to how the abdominal muscles are working.

In this exercise, you are in an elongated position, with your spine in line, and the abdomen does not move toward the pelvis. The ERV is produced by the abdominal muscles, which cause the abdomen to rise toward the thorax.

Exercise 3: Global anterior diaphragmatic inhalation using the entire belly in the front

You just worked with a movement that causes the abdomen to sink inward. Now notice the movement that occurs naturally during the inhalation that follows. Your abdomen, which sank inward during exhalation, now bulges forward as you inhale.

Let this movement happen, and let it progressively flow through your abdomen at the area where it is easiest, that is, at the front. Be sure that this is a comfortable movement for your body.

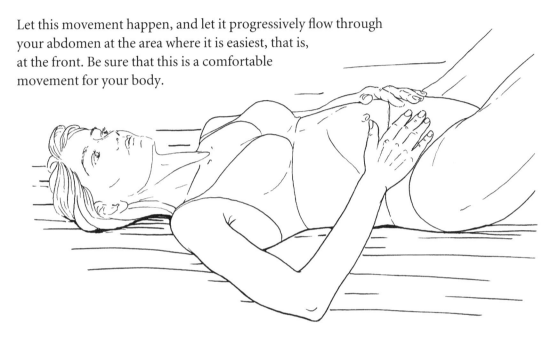

Remember what theoretically happens at this moment: The diaphragm descends toward the pelvis, which deforms the abdomen in the area where it is most evident — the front — at about the level of the navel.

Try to recognize the area, but also the duration of this movement. Can you do the same type of inhalation using a smaller amplitude of IRV? Can you do it with a bigger amplitude?

Then, try to feel the same movement when you are inhaling a very small volume of air.

This inhalation exercise, where you neither concentrate on a specific area of the abdomen nor direct the pushing force toward a specific site, works on the entire abdomen, which is why it is called *global* anterior diaphragmatic breathing.

This is the most obvious type of diaphragmatic inhalation, and is the first exercise practiced in breathing technique classes. It is done to enhance breathing, singing, speaking, and relaxation.

Note: Most people are unable to do this first type of coordination—contraction of the diaphragm/release of the abdominals. Instead, they usually do one of the following:

• They do another type of breathing:

—They immediately perform the respiratory movement in the costal area. They open their ribs in a variety of ways, often because they worry about doing it right, and because the rib area is more easily felt than the diaphragm; sometimes because it is not accepted in their culture to "stick out your belly."

—Or they perform a so-called "paradoxical" inhalation. The ribs open so much that the lungs are stretched. They start rising from the base and pull the abdominal mass along with them. *The belly sinks inward a lot during inhalation, while the ribs open up at the same time* (see page 144). Consequently, during exhalation, the ribs close and the abdomen moves downward and bulges out. This type of breathing is the opposite of diaphragmatic breathing.

• They produce a similar movement:

Some people will arch their lumbar spine to make the abdomen bulge out. In this case, the movement of the abdomen is not due to the pushing of the diaphragm, but to the contraction of the back muscles.

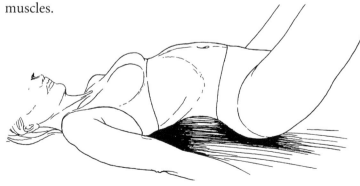

This occurs most frequently when the exercise is performed in an upright position. That is why it is important to start working with the back totally "glued" to the floor.

When you are able to do this first "global" breathing well, you should be able to repeat it easily, stop and start it again, and work it at different rates of speed and with different amplitudes. At this point, you can proceed to change the form.

Now you want the pushing of the diaphragm, combined with the reaction of the abdominals, to affect other parts of the abdomen. You can affect the higher and lower parts, as well as the sides toward the front and the back. You can even push toward the perineum.

All of this breathing is diaphragmatic breathing (1ST mechanism). It can also be distinguished according to the part of the abdomen that is deformed.

Exercise 4: *Diaphragmatic inhalation at different abdominal levels*

Place both hands on the abdomen, one in the area above the pubic bone, the other in the area of the epigastrium.

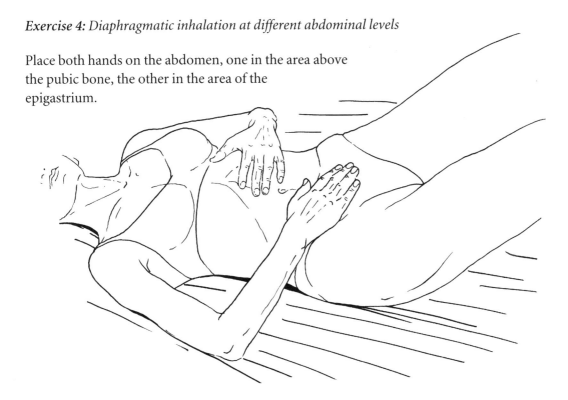

Repeat your diaphragmatic breathing. Focus your attention on the areas below the two hands and note which of these moves more during inhalation.

The upper one? The lower one?

Again, just observe here.

Which hand moves more may vary depending on factors like stress, fatigue, digestion, and so forth. It is therefore normal if you find that this differs from day to day.

Now, interfere with your breathing again by causing movement under just one of your hands.

Start by keeping the lower hand (just above the pubic bone) as still as possible, and the movement there at a minimum. At the same time, try to make the area under the upper hand (above the navel) bulge out progressively 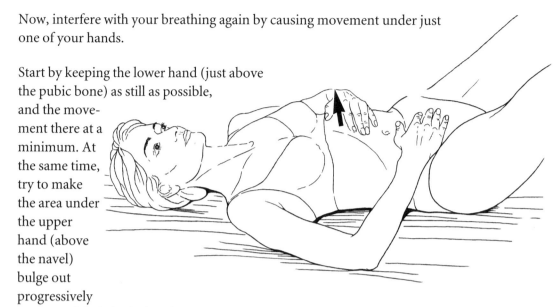 more until, little by little, it becomes more full here and is the only area that has movement.

Then, try to reverse the level of the abdomen that moves. This time it is not the area under your upper hand (epigastrium) that is bulging with each inhalation, but the area under the lower hand (above the pubic bone).

Here again, try to make this lower area bulge out progressively more — even if it feels as if you are "pushing" toward this area — all the while making sure that there is no movement in the upper area.

To adapt your breathing to different levels may take several days of practice. So don't be surprised if you don't achieve an immediate result: Like every coordination, this one will require some training.

Exercise 5: Anterior diaphragmatic inhalation, with pushing toward the back

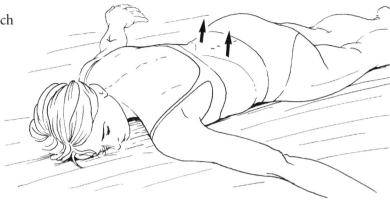

Lie down on your stomach and repeat the last breathing exercise. At the moment where your abdomen would normally go forward, the movement is stopped by the resistance of the floor.

The movement is then sent back to the back of the trunk. Can you feel how your lumbar spine is lifted up by the "push" from the floor?

Take time to really familiarize yourself with this movement, and to be able to identify it. Try it often. In this exercise, the back does not become round because of the stomach moving inward. Rather, the diaphragm pushes forward. The counter-pressure of the floor reflects this push backward and causes the back to become round, reducing or even eliminating its natural curve at the lumbar spine.

These inhalations are very effective for mobilizing the spine in a gentle way. They are especially good for maintaining and enhancing smooth motion of the lumbar spine.

This exercise could be part of a series of movements to mobilize the entire spine.

After this, you can modify these movements in two ways:

- You can change the level where the movement is done, either higher or lower on the spine.

  If the movement is done very low (just above the pubic bone), it causes anterior tilting of the pelvis and produces a lordosis of the lower lumbar spine.

  If the movement is done at a higher level (at L1-L3), it typically brings the lumbar spine out of lordosis.

- You can produce the movement more on either side of the lumbar spine, which causes a slightly asymmetrical mobilization.

Exercise 6: *Posterior diaphragmatic inhalation*

Visualize your abdominal cavity and its borders again. Now imagine that the pushing of the diaphragm changes the back of your abdomen. During inhalation, your back is rounded and, in a manner of speaking, glued to the floor, giving itself even more support.

Here the thrust of the diaphragm is headed directly toward the back (1) because it moves it there, and (2) because your abdominals stay in tonic contraction and prevent the abdomen from bulging forward.

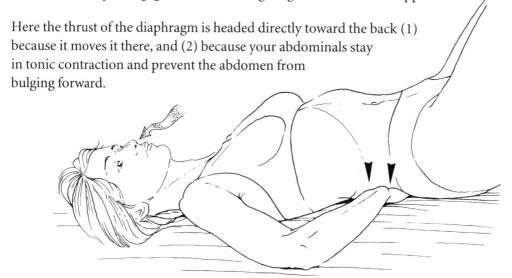

You can also place a hand or a fairly thin piece of foam under your back. Now, push into the hand or foam with your lumbar area.

If this breathing movement is hard to find, change your starting position:

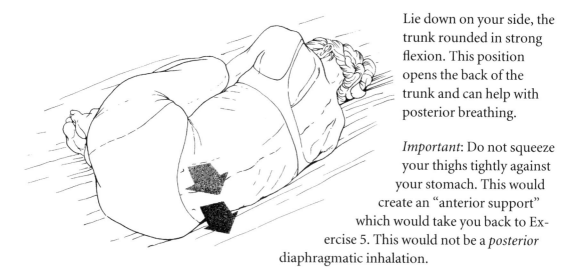

Lie down on your side, the trunk rounded in strong flexion. This position opens the back of the trunk and can help with posterior breathing.

Important: Do not squeeze your thighs tightly against your stomach. This would create an "anterior support" which would take you back to Exercise 5. This would not be a *posterior* diaphragmatic inhalation.

As described in the preceding exercises, you can do this posterior push higher up in your abdomen (the back of your lower ribs) or lower (in the back of the iliac fossae).

Exercise 7: Asymmetrical diaphragmatic inhalation

Now, place your hands slightly to the right or left of the navel. Do not place them on your hips. They should still be on the front of the abdomen.

Take a breath in tidal volume and focus on the movement of your abdomen. Is the movement totally symmetrical or does it dominate on one side?

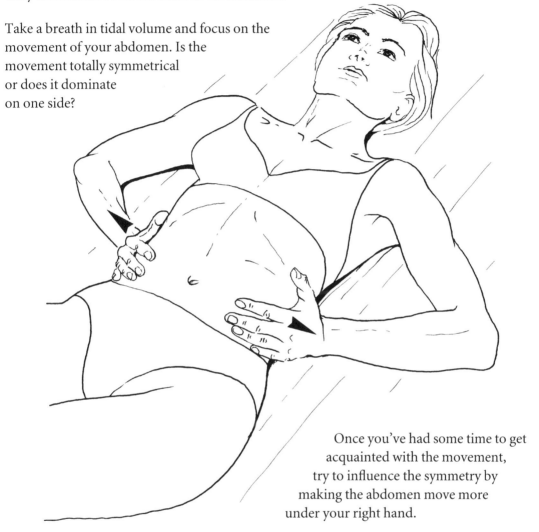

Once you've had some time to get acquainted with the movement, try to influence the symmetry by making the abdomen move more under your right hand.

As with breathing on different levels, try to progressively make the movement happen *only* on the right, with greater amplitude.

When you've familiarized yourself with this movement, try the other side.

Later, when you are able to do these asymmetrical movements at the waist, try them at different levels. For example, you can place the hands lower (in the right and left iliac fossae) or higher (above the navel, to each side of the midline).

This exercise of controlling the movement of the diaphragm can help you selectively mobilize specific abdominal organs.

Exercise 8: Perineal diaphragmatic inhalation

You can also make the diaphragm push directly downward toward the perineal area. (For practical reasons, you should first use the toilet before doing this exercise.)

Lie down on your back with the hips, knees, and ankles flexed, and both feet flat on the floor (as on page 176). Now try to make your diaphragm descend without causing the stomach, back, or sides of the trunk to bulge outward.

Can you feel that the only area where you can now direct the pressure is the lowest area on your trunk, the bottom of your pelvis? This is the perineum.

Your perineum can react in several different ways:

- The most familiar response is the *sphincter response*. Usually, when you push toward the perineum, you open one or both sphincters to urinate or have a bowel movement.

- There is also the response of the pelvic floor, which is located, like a "little diaphragm," at the bottom of your abdominal cavity. This muscular "hammock" can react in different ways, that is, with varying tonicity.

Now try to feel the perineal area when you press downward:

- This area can contract strongly, without being deformed by the pressure. This is what happens when you exert yourself, for example, when you lift an object or when you "push."

- This area can also relax totally, slackening under the pressure.

Between these two extremes, there is a wide variety of nuanced responses. You can do this exercise while inhaling or exhaling. It is something you do very often while urinating, defecating, and, in women, while pushing during the birthing process.

This is why it is important that you empty your bowels and bladder before you begin this exercise.

Diaphragmatic inhalation — 2nd mechanism

Here, the diaphragm is always active while the abdomen does not move. The central tendon is fixed. The action of the diaphragm raises the ribs at the bottom edge of the thoracic cage and makes them move apart.

You can do this exercise while lying on the floor or while standing.

Exercise 1: Lateral diaphragmatic inhalation

Place your hands on the sides of the ribs, just above the waist. Make sure you position them at the bottom of the ribs and not in the area below the armpits. With both hands, press into the ribs (similar to the exercise described on page 162). Feel how this narrows the thorax.

During the next inhalation, keep the hands pressed against the rib cage and have the ribs push them back. After two or three seconds, relax the hands and feel how the ribs move apart and rise in a large movement.

Exercise 2: Anterior diaphragmatic inhalation

Now put both hands closer to the front above the epigastrium, on the edge of the costal cartilage at the costal angle.

Inhale and try to move your ribs under your hands. Can you feel the movement? The sternum rises. The costal cartilages rise and move slightly apart.

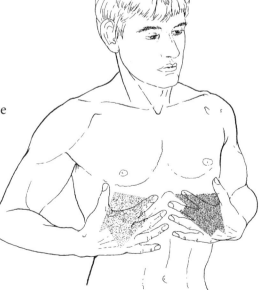

Exercise 2, cont.

Feel how the momentum of this movement comes from the interior of the thorax (and not from the exterior). In fact, the pectoralis major produces a similar movement. The difference is that the pectoralis major produces the movement from the outside of the thorax. If you do this exercise while lying on the floor, feel how the back stays in contact with the floor so that the sternum does not protrude by arching the back. (That would be an inhalation using the back muscles; see page 92.)

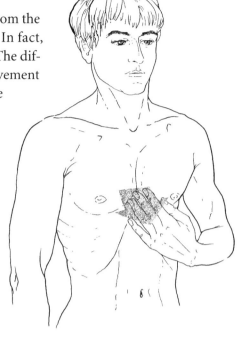

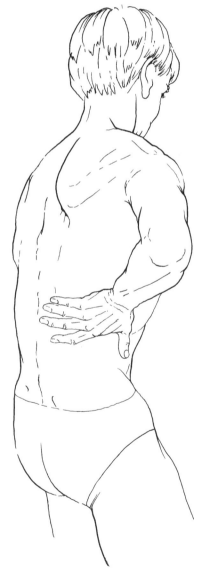

Exercise 3: Posterior diaphragmatic inhalation

Now move both hands to the back of the trunk and place them under the lowest ribs. If you do this exercise on your back, you can also place a small piece of foam the size of a sponge, or a small towel folded in quarters, in this area.

Inhale into your ribs in this area and try to make them push back your hands. This inhalation is very similar to the one described on page 184. In this area of the trunk, the two mechanisms are difficult to distinguish.

COSTAL INHALATION

The following breathing movements involve the *upper part of the trunk*. As with diaphragmatic inhalation, there is a great variety of movements.

On the next few pages, we will present breathing exercises muscle by muscle, where every costal inspiratory muscle is dealt with separately.

Then, we will show you breathing movements which enlist a group of several muscles working at the same time, and involve the entire thoracic cage.

All costal inhalations, even though they are presented separately for the purpose of practice, can of course be mixed and combined with the diaphragmatic inhalations shown on the preceding pages. They can be exercised with different respiratory volumes and at different rates of speed.

Recommendations for the practice of costal inhalation

1. First, get to know these exercises. Then, to develop a specific muscle action, you can practice *successive inhalations* by creating "stepped" apneas:

    a. Inhale tidal volume.

    b. Stop breathing for a moment.

    c. Inhale a larger volume.

    d. Hold the breath for a short while.

    e. If you can, inhale an even larger volume.

    f. Relax completely.

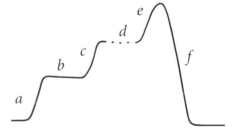

2. Make sure you respect the time needed to *exhale*, which must be completed (even going into ERV at times):

    • Avoid starting to inhale again too early, which happens often in costal breathing and can produce hyperventilation (causing lightheadedness).

    • Make the thorax move in both directions, closing as well as opening it.

Costal breathing can sometimes mobilize areas of the lungs that are not well ventilated. It also often goes hand in hand with an increase in tonus.

Exercise 1: *Inhaling under the clavicle using your pectoralis minor*

> This is a basic exercise, which can release the upper part of the chest and free up the shoulders.

The beginning of this exercise will enable you to visualize the area of the pectoralis minor.

Sit down on a chair the height of a stool, close to a wall. Lean with your back against the wall. Then move the left shoulder off the wall by turning toward your right. Only your right shoulder blade now leans against the wall.

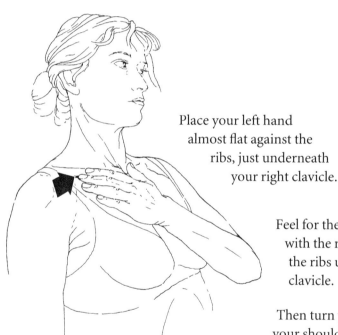

Place your left hand almost flat against the ribs, just underneath your right clavicle.

Feel for the clavicle with your fingertips, and with the rest of your hand, feel the area of the ribs underneath and slightly deep to the clavicle.

Then turn your attention to the contact of your shoulder blade against the wall.

Now try to get a clear visual image of the space between the wall, the shoulder blade pressing against the wall (through your clothes), and the space behind the upper ribs against your hand. In this area, the front and back of the body are not parallel, as you would think. The shoulder blade and the top of the ribs at the back are at a 45 degree angle with respect to the outline of the ribs in the front. This space corresponds to the portion of the lungs located at almost the top of the lungs. This area is seldom mobilized. (The ribs are often mobilized, but not that high in the body.) That is why you should not be surprised if it takes quite a while to find movement and breathing in this area.

Can you perceive breathing movements in the front or back of this area in your body? While paying attention to the movement in the front, can you move it so that the back always stays in contact with the wall?

Now, can you make these movements open and close the ribs? This will cause a high costal respiration.

Then try to progressively increase the amplitude of this movement. Make an inhalation of IRV of medium amplitude. Try to hold this amplitude without breathing. Then exhale with the highest possible amplitude, so that you become aware of the contrast between inhalation and exhalation in this posture.

At the front, your hand is in contact with your pectoralis major, but the muscle that lifts your upper ribs in this area is the pectoralis minor, which is located below the pectoralis major. During inhalation, the underlying layer of the pectoralis minor contracts and lifts the first few ribs, located below your hand.

Make sure your right arm and shoulder are relaxed and do not participate in the movement, so that the movement is clearly felt *in the ribs*, and not in the shoulder.

Now repeat this exercise on the other side. Afterwards, you may want to try to make both areas work together, on each side of the upper sternum, and to feel how the upper part of the chest just underneath the clavicles opens up.

While you are working with this area, pay attention to the corresponding movement in the back. Avoid compensating for the opening movement of the upper ribs with a closing movement of the lumbar spine in the back, which can tighten this area. This is especially true when you work both sides at the same time.

Before doing this exercise, you can perform a relaxation exercise for the shoulder by stretching the pectoral muscles (see page 170).

The reverse is also possible: You can do this breathing exercise before stretching the pectoral muscles. Breathing into the upper part of the thorax is an effective preparation for relaxing these muscles.

With this exercise, you also mobilize a part of the lungs that is not ventilated very much. This type of breathing also often goes hand in hand with an increase in tonus.

Exercise 2: *Inhaling while opening the chest to the front using the pectoralis major*

The pectoralis major muscle spreads out across the top part of the chest.

In women, this muscle is located almost entirely under the breast. It completely covers the pectoralis minor and reaches out above it in all directions.

Stand upright with your back against the wall (similar to the pectoralis minor exercise), but this time, instead of leaning the shoulder blade against the wall, lean the area above the shoulder blade against the wall.

To do this, pull your shoulders back completely so that you lean with your entire back against the wall. At this point, the shoulder blades move away from the wall. You can also do this exercise while lying on the floor.

In order to engage the inspiratory action of the pectoralis major, you must first locate the insertion of the muscle at two places:

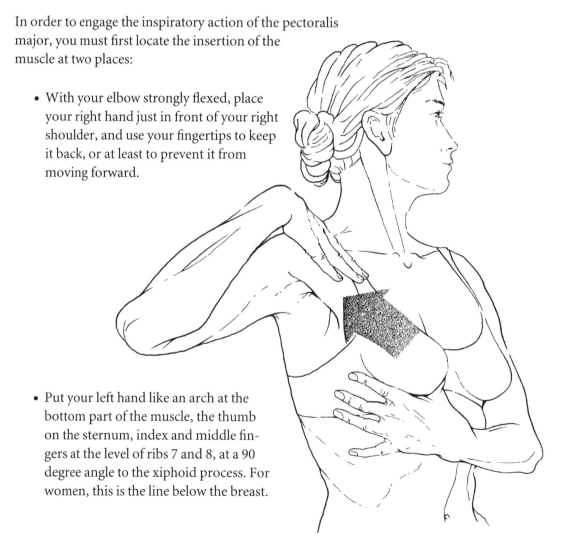

- With your elbow strongly flexed, place your right hand just in front of your right shoulder, and use your fingertips to keep it back, or at least to prevent it from moving forward.

- Put your left hand like an arch at the bottom part of the muscle, the thumb on the sternum, index and middle fingers at the level of ribs 7 and 8, at a 90 degree angle to the xiphoid process. For women, this is the line below the breast.

Keep the back of your ribs in contact with the wall and check to see if there is a movement in your ribs against your left hand.

Does this area lift or move apart when you inhale?

Exhale and let the movement reverse itself. This helps you find the place where the movement occurs. Can you discover the amplitude at this place? It is usually easier here than in the area of the pectoralis minor, since the ribs are freer and larger in this area.

Make sure that you keep your back in contact with the wall so that you do not replace the movement of the ribs with an arching of the thoracic spine. This would involve the work of the back muscles rather than the pectoral muscles.

Keep your shoulders straight across the top of the thorax. If you are able, keep your right hand in front of the shoulder during this exercise to make sure that the shoulder does not move forward.

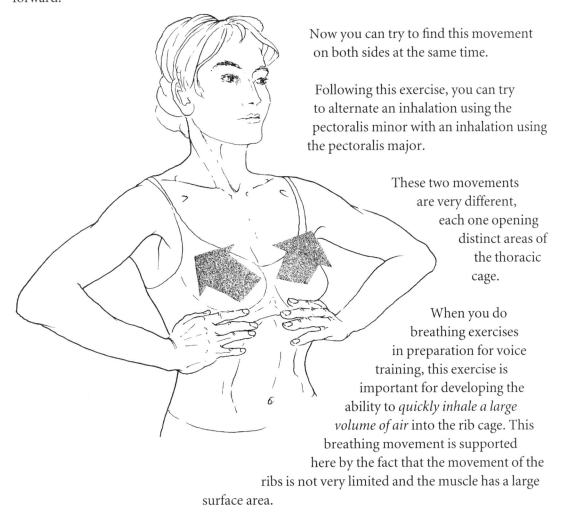

Now you can try to find this movement on both sides at the same time.

Following this exercise, you can try to alternate an inhalation using the pectoralis minor with an inhalation using the pectoralis major.

These two movements are very different, each one opening distinct areas of the thoracic cage.

When you do breathing exercises in preparation for voice training, this exercise is important for developing the ability to *quickly inhale a large volume of air* into the rib cage. This breathing movement is supported here by the fact that the movement of the ribs is not very limited and the muscle has a large surface area.

Exercise 3: Inhaling by opening the ribs under the arm using the serratus anterior

This is the most expansive of all the costal inhalation techniques.

Stand upright without leaning against the wall. Bend your elbows and place your hands on the sides of the ribs, as high up as you can. Use either the palm of your hand or the finger joints, whatever works best.

Let the weight of your arms fall onto the ribs and observe how this weight presses on the ribs and bends them, making your thorax more narrow.

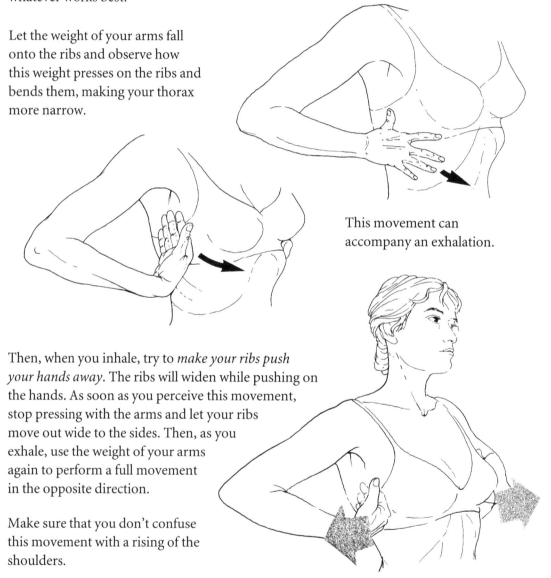

This movement can accompany an exhalation.

Then, when you inhale, try to *make your ribs push your hands away*. The ribs will widen while pushing on the hands. As soon as you perceive this movement, stop pressing with the arms and let your ribs move out wide to the sides. Then, as you exhale, use the weight of your arms again to perform a full movement in the opposite direction.

Make sure that you don't confuse this movement with a rising of the shoulders.

Do you feel how the inhalation is large and goes to the side, with almost no movement to the front? It allows you to inhale a very large volume of air. It is also a good exercise to alternate with pectoral breathing, which mostly (and sometimes even too much) develops the anterior aspect of the respiratory movement.

Exercise 4: Inhaling by arching your back using the back muscles

Inhale deeply (big IRV) into the front using the pectoralis major muscles (as described on page 192), so that the anterior part of the thorax opens wide.

Relax, exhale, and repeat this type of inhalation. Now observe the back of your rib cage instead of the front. If you have done this in a very spontaneous fashion, without trying to correct anything, do you feel how the back has closed, compressing on itself, while the front has opened?

The ribs have moved closer together and, most importantly, the thoracic spine is brought into extension, causing the spinous processes of the vertebrae to move closer together.

This last movement can be a passive one, where the vertebrae follow the movement of the rib cage and adapt to its form. But it can also be very active, where the curving of the back muscles causes the opening of the ribs in the front.

Now, try to arch your back only in the thoracic area. Be sure not to arch the waist or bring back your shoulders.

Try to move the spinous processes of your spine as closely together as possible and be aware of how this movement modifies your ribs in the front. There, you will feel an opening, which resembles what was done with the pectoralis major muscles. They are similar only in form though, not in the sensation you feel. In this movement, you use the muscles of the back of the spine without contracting any muscle in the front.

This closing in of the back, which can be more or less active, often accompanies anterior breathing in beginners. Depending on the case, you may choose to let the breathing happen this way just because it is such a spontaneous movement, or you may try to prevent it, if you wish to accompany the opening in the front with a similar opening in the back.

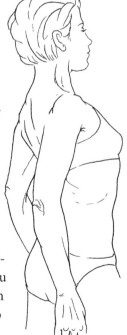

Exercise 5: *Inhaling while opening the ribs in the back using the levatores costarum muscles*

These inhalations mobilize the back of the ribs. It is not easy to feel breathing in this area because it is in the back, and breathing is usually visualized and practiced in the front. To find this movement, you need to put your thoracic cage in a very rounded position (thoracic kyphosis). For example, take a sitting position with the back bent forward, supported by your hands, thighs, pillow, etc. (see page 212); or use the side-lying position, with the back rolled in; or (as is shown here), kneel with your back bent completely forward, possibly resting on a pillow.

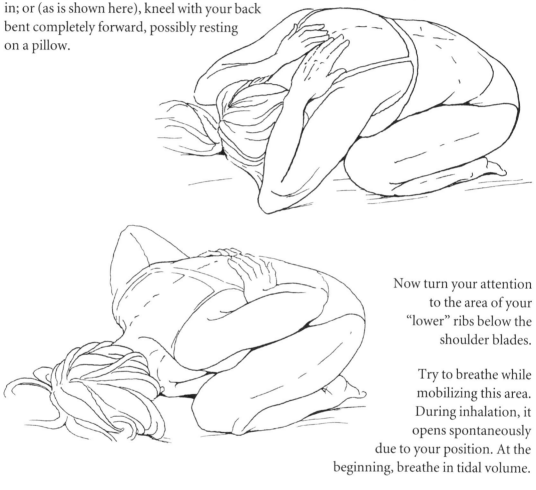

Now turn your attention to the area of your "lower" ribs below the shoulder blades.

Try to breathe while mobilizing this area. During inhalation, it opens spontaneously due to your position. At the beginning, breathe in tidal volume.

Imagine that someone "brushes your sides against the grain" (upward) as you inhale. During exhalation, feel how the ribs automatically return to their original position. Repeat this several times while breathing in tidal volume. Then, try to boost the amplitude during inhalation. Always let this area fall back automatically during exhalation.

Mobilizing the top ribs

Now, elongate an arm by bringing it forward. Place the second hand over the first. By moving the arms this way, you raise the shoulder blade and the ribs higher up.

Continue to inhale toward the back, but this time into these high ribs. They move much less (see page 46). This area may even be painful and stiff. Try to increase these movements gradually over the course of several sessions. Little by little, you can try to boost the amplitude of the movement and find the breathing in all the posterior ribs, while alternating the level and respiratory volume.

Later, when you are very familiar with the mobility in the back, you can try to reproduce this in positions that are not bent forward — for example, standing, lying on your back or on your stomach, and so forth.

Exercise 6: Inhaling through the top and back using the serratus posterior superior

Now, palpate the back of your neck, placing your fingers on the spinous processes of the cervical spine. In the middle of the neck, the spinous processes (C4 and C5) are very short. They are much longer at the base of the neck. Place your fingertips on each side of the spinous processes at the base of the neck (C6 through T1), that is, a little below the curve of the neck.

Now imagine that you inhale by lifting the highest ribs at the back by contracting the muscles located where your fingers are.

The muscles that are involved here are the serratus posterior superior.

Posterior breathing in this area is minimal considering the size of the ribs. Try to find it anyway. This breathing is very important to help mobilize this area of the vertebrae and ribs, even if it is a minimal mobilization.

Exercise 7: Inhaling in the top front using the sternocleidomastoid (SCM)

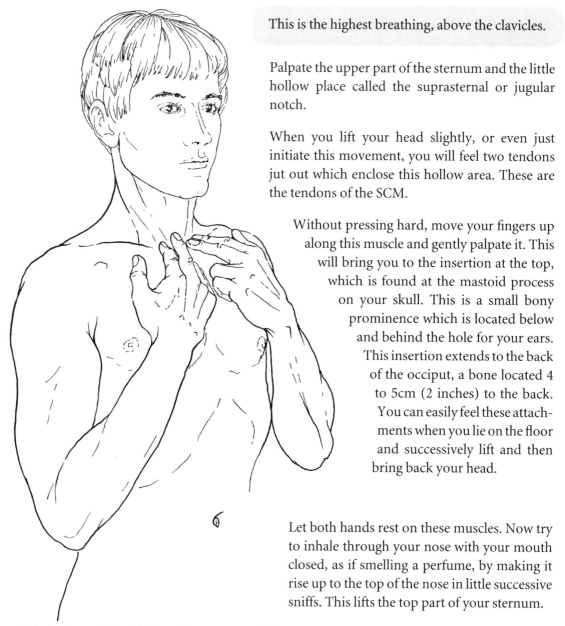

This is the highest breathing, above the clavicles.

Palpate the upper part of the sternum and the little hollow place called the suprasternal or jugular notch.

When you lift your head slightly, or even just initiate this movement, you will feel two tendons jut out which enclose this hollow area. These are the tendons of the SCM.

Without pressing hard, move your fingers up along this muscle and gently palpate it. This will bring you to the insertion at the top, which is found at the mastoid process on your skull. This is a small bony prominence which is located below and behind the hole for your ears. This insertion extends to the back of the occiput, a bone located 4 to 5cm (2 inches) to the back. You can easily feel these attachments when you lie on the floor and successively lift and then bring back your head.

Let both hands rest on these muscles. Now try to inhale through your nose with your mouth closed, as if smelling a perfume, by making it rise up to the top of the nose in little successive sniffs. This lifts the top part of your sternum.

This is almost like inhaling "into your neck." Can you feel the contraction of the SCM? Can you also feel how this contraction is not necessarily symmetrical? Repeat this several times to experience the sensation.

You can also inhale a large quantity of air here (IRV). However, do not continue doing this type of breathing for too long because it can cause tension at the neck and shoulders if practiced continuously.

Exercise 8: Inhaling at the top, but more laterally, using the scalenes

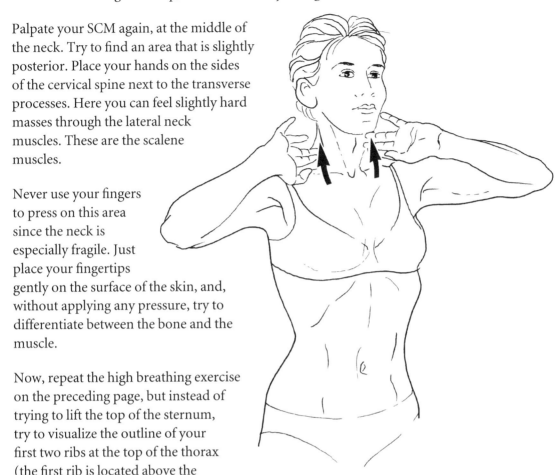

Palpate your SCM again, at the middle of the neck. Try to find an area that is slightly posterior. Place your hands on the sides of the cervical spine next to the transverse processes. Here you can feel slightly hard masses through the lateral neck muscles. These are the scalene muscles.

Never use your fingers to press on this area since the neck is especially fragile. Just place your fingertips gently on the surface of the skin, and, without applying any pressure, try to differentiate between the bone and the muscle.

Now, repeat the high breathing exercise on the preceding page, but instead of trying to lift the top of the sternum, try to visualize the outline of your first two ribs at the top of the thorax (the first rib is located above the clavicle) and imagine that you are trying to lift this first rib from the sides, like a bucket handle.

The movement here is much more restricted than in the lower rib area because:

- The ribs are much smaller.

- The costal cartilage is much shorter.

- At this level, the axis of articulation between the rib and vertebra allows sagittal movements more readily than lateral movements.

Therefore, do not be surprised that the movement here allows only minimal amplitude. Inhale very high and attempt an IRV in this area, but do it in little steps, as if you were to successively inhale about ten gasps of air. After four or five inhalations, can you feel the scalenes contract under your fingers? Now, exhale and take several normal breaths anywhere else in your trunk so that you don't tense up with too many high inhalations.

COSTAL EXHALATIONS

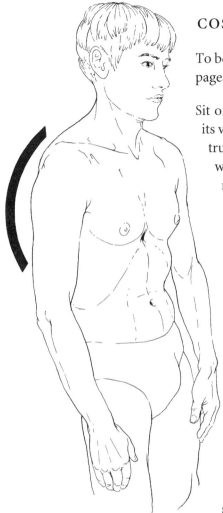

To become aware of the exhalations described in the following pages, prepare in the following manner:

Sit on a chair or stand upright and sense your erect trunk in its vertical position. Now, slump down a little bit and let your trunk "fall" slightly forward, as you would do spontaneously when you are tired (keep looking forward throughout this movement).

As you do this, the ribs are lowered and the sternum moves backward so that the thoracic cage closes up in an expiratory position.

As you will see from this experience, the most spontaneous costal exhalation is accompanied by a slight bending of the spine. This movement is due to gravity.

Repeat this type of exhalation several times. Can you feel what volume you are exhaling? You can exhale a little more strongly than tidal volume to start working in slight ERV.

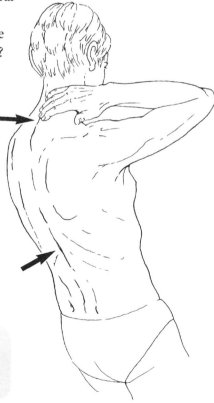

Now locate the areas where the spine bends: at the top of the ribs/the base of the neck (C7/T1), at the bottom of the ribs, above the waist (T11 through L1).

Thus, the bending occurs in the two transitional areas of the spine: the cervicothoracic and thoracolumbar regions.

This method of exhaling is very natural and brings back a spontaneous quality to your breathing. It works well together with the sigh.

Exercise 1: Lowering the ribs using the abdominal muscles

Now, try to breathe out more using the same movement. You must lower the ribs even further. First, try to move the xiphoid process of the sternum. Your thoracic cage will flatten slightly. This movement works with the rectus abdominis muscle.

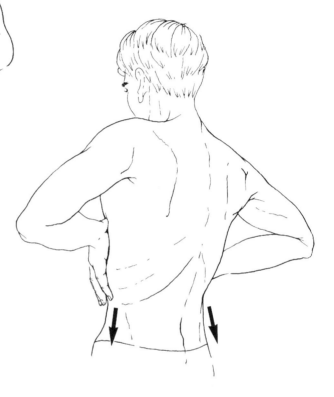

Then try to lower your ribs on the sides at the waist. Your thoracic cage narrows. This movement works with the obliques. In both cases, can you feel how the lowering of the ribs is accompanied by a flexion of the spine from T11 through L1?

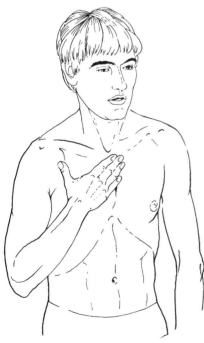

Exercise 2: Lowering the ribs using the transversus thoracis

Place your hand on the top half of the sternum. Try to find the movement by pulling back this area of the bone while letting the xiphoid process stay behind. This movement works with the transversus thoracis. Can you feel how this action is accompanied by a flexion of the spine, but this time at the level of C7/T1?

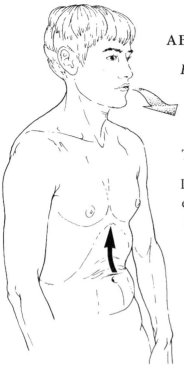

ABDOMINAL EXHALATIONS

Exercise 1: *Sucking in the top part of the abdomen*

Stand upright and repeat the movement at the beginning of the previous page. Let your spine slump down. At the same time, try to breathe out *without lowering your ribs.* This mobilizes the stomach.

Do you notice how exhaling into the epigastric area comes very easily? This is also the most obvious movement. The belly is sucked into the entire area under the costal angle.

The location of this movement is almost the same as during low costal exhalation. However, the movement itself is different. You don't try to close the ribs, but to suck in the belly upward.

Try to do a quick, strong exhalation in the following manner: Pretend you let the breath exit directly from your stomach.

This exhalation, where the movement controls the mid-trunk, is very easy to find. It is associated with a flexion of the spine, which occurs in the same area, as we saw on the previous page. You can practice this every time you work with spontaneous breathing techniques.

You can also use this type of breathing when you want to feel how your abdomen is involved in exhalation during voice training with your natural voice.

Next, try to repeat the same type of exhalation *without curving your spine.* Exhale as completely as you can. Place one hand on the lower part of the abdomen. This area should not participate during a complete exhalation using the mid-trunk area. It may even bulge because some of the pressure from the epigastric area pushes on the abdomen. There may also be some pressure toward the perineum.

This may seem like a bad or improper breathing exercise. Indeed, it is, *if your expiration in ERV is always produced this way.* That is why it is important to practice exhaling by using the abdominal muscles "from bottom to top," as described on the following page.

Exercise 2: *Rising abdominal exhalation*

In this type of exhalation, you successively contract the different levels of the abdomen, starting from the bottom and working your way up to the top. At each new level, make sure that you maintain the contraction of the levels below.

Step 1: Contract the perineal area.

Start by contracting your anus in order to feel the back of your pelvic floor. Now, try to contract the entire area in the front. (This is not the same as a contraction of the buttocks or the abdominals, but a contraction in the depth of your pelvis.)

Repeat this several times while alternating contraction and relaxation.

Step 2: Add to this a contraction of the lower region of the abdomen.

This area is still quite a bit lower than the waist, which you have not yet contracted. Try to first contract the perineum (Step 1) and then this area (Step 2). As you perform these two successive contractions, exhale a starting volume of ERV.

If it is helpful, breathe out while doing a small occlusive in the mouth by making the sound "*ffff*" or "*ssss.*"

Before you continue with Step 3, make sure that you master the first two steps. This may take several days.

Step 3: Add a contraction that reaches up to the level of the waist.

Note: When you arrive at waist level, the movement will be *dominated by a contraction of the transversus abdominis* and you may lose the contraction of the perineum. This is because the transversus strongly tightens the abdomen at the waist, exerting strong pressure below.

It may take some time to master this step. Do not be afraid to go back to Steps 1 and 2 before adding Step 3. You can also add an exhalation in ERV to the abdominal movement of Step 3, possibly by forming the sound "*ffff*" or "*ssss.*"

Step 4: Let the contraction go up to the top of the epigastrium.

Do this exercise without losing the contractions at the levels below. The contraction of the transversus abdominis is still the most dominant contraction. That is why you have to make sure that you maintain the lower contractions, especially the contraction of the perineum.

This technique is very effective for strengthening the lower part of the abdomen, but it is rarely a spontaneous movement. It usually requires a progressive learning phase at the beginning and, later on, continued practice to maintain it.

EXERCISES FOR RESPIRATORY VOLUMES

As we have seen throughout the book, breathing can be practiced with different volumes of air, and these volumes in turn influence the forces involved in producing respiratory movements.

Different types of breathing can be classified according to the specific volume used.

In this chapter, we will walk through a systematic exercise for each of these volumes. Although they can occur at different parts of the body (high, low, anterior, posterior, etc.), only some of them will be described here.

We will also discuss each of these volumes to show you how volumes can be strung together in a variety of ways, just like a musical score or the text of a lecture.

At the end of the chapter, you will find several typical examples where different volumes will create a type of breathing that is completely different from the normal way of breathing given the forces involved.

Experimenting with tidal volume

For this exercise, it is best to place yourself
in a relaxed position, stretched out comfortably.

Observe your breathing, its rhythm, amplitude,
and its reduced muscle action.

Your body does not need a lot of oxygen at this point.

Does your breathing cause a lot of movement?

And are these movements visible to another person?

Where in your body do these movements occur?

Is the volume of airflow the same from one breath to the next?

Changing the area involved

Can you make the respiratory movements occur in your belly, high up in the ribs, or around your waist? Make sure that you are still in tidal volume.

Inhalation in tidal volume

Pay attention to how the intake of air begins gradually during this inhalation. You don't need a great amount of air, so you don't need to rush the movement.

The inspiratory muscles (especially the diaphragm) work in a very smooth manner, adapting themselves as much as possible to the neurological commands which calculate the gas content of the blood.

They meet with progressive resistance from pulmonary elasticity, which also increases gradually, but in a moderate fashion.

Apnea following an inhalation

This is a short time of suspension. The forces involved in breathing are still present. The maximum volume has been reached and a release of the forces is imminent. This is a brief, tonic apnea, which is very different from the one experienced following an exhalation.

Exhalation in tidal volume

Feel how the forces involved in exhalation change. First, the airflow is fast, then it decelerates. This is due to the fact that the elastic recoil force of the lungs is stronger at the beginning of an exhalation than at the end. Toward the end, the lungs become more relaxed until they have returned to their original shape, where there is no elastic force. This relaxed state continues without interruption through the start of the apnea that follows.

Apnea following an exhalation

Observe the apnea that follows the exhalation (or sigh) in tidal volume. The airflow has stopped. Are you able to extend this moment until its completion without trying to catch air too quickly, so that the body can do what it needs to do?

How do you feel at this moment? How does your body feel leaning against the floor? How is your body tone?

Do you feel as if your entire body is like a tuning fork reflecting the relaxed tone of the inspiratory muscles?

It is essential to experiment with this state of relaxation of your muscles. This is like a "sensory landmark" that you will be able to recognize later in the course of your daily life, a moment of relaxation.

Note that during times of stress, you will have the tendency to shorten this time of apnea and to start inhaling too quickly again (see "Panting" on page 149).

Experimenting with Inspiratory Reserve Volume (IRV)

IRV linked to physical effort

An easy way to inhale IRV is to boost the speed and intensity of your physical effort. For example, you can run as fast as possible for a few minutes, or dance at a buoyant rhythm, or bicycle quickly uphill.

During this effort, you mostly increase the *frequency* of your breathing. Once you stop and recuperate, you increase the *amplitude* of your breathing — you spontaneously take deeper breaths. The mouth is often open in order to inhale the largest amount of air possible (see page 77). You are then working in IRV.

IRV without physical effort

Apart from the IRV linked to physical effort, you can experiment with this volume for reasons other than just the gas exchange. You may want to strengthen certain inspiratory muscles, enlarge the rib cage, make the intercostals more flexible, and so forth.

However, if your body exerts practically no muscular effort, inhalation in IRV can quickly lead to hyperventilation. Remember to always alternate one or two inhalations of IRV with several breaths of tidal volume. This can help you avoid hyperventilation, which can sometimes lead to uncomfortable side effects, like dizziness.

Step-by-step inhalation in IRV

Start by breathing normally in tidal volume.

The next time you inhale, try to breathe in as much air as you can. Persist until you achieve what you believe to be your maximum inhalation quantity.

When you have reached that volume, stop breathing (apnea).

Inhale again and hold your breath.

Now inhale yet another time.

Finally, release all the air by breathing out.

Go back to breathing in tidal volume.

This method of inhaling in steps helps you develop efficient IRV breathing without becoming hyperventilated.

The apneas are very active to keep the lungs in an open position.

IRV while breathing into your ribs

Can you inhale deeply into your ribs by successively opening different areas of the rib cage? For example, the front, the front top and bottom, then the sides, then the back, the bottom back, and finally the top back. Now relax and take several spontaneous breaths.

IRV while breathing into your abdomen

Exhale as completely as possible. Then inhale while letting your belly bulge out. Do not hold back, but let your abdomen go forward as much as possible (see page 179).

Exhalation in IRV

Take a deep breath in again. Notice the exhalation that follows. It resembles a very deep release. It is done very quickly, especially at the beginning.

If the inhalation was very deep, you should be able to notice the glottis tighten up spontaneously to "hold back" the rate of speed during the exhalation that follows.

Holding the exhalation in IRV

Try to slow down the exhalation of IRV as much as possible by keeping the glottis wide open. There are two ways to achieve this. Can you feel them? You can either try to move the ribs apart while exhaling (which may make the belly move inward), or you can keep the belly bulging out slightly. Of course, you can also do both at the same time.

Apneas after returning from IRV

Repeat the preceding breathing exercise. During the exhalation, stop completely without closing your glottis (keep your mouth and glottis open).

Do you feel the tension in this apnea? This is not a pause, like in the apnea of tidal volume. Instead, it is an active apnea. It can even be very active when you do it at the beginning of the exhalation in IRV.

You should be able to feel the force of the muscles either in the ribs or at the top of the abdomen, while the diaphragm stays contracted in order to slow down its own lifting.

Experimenting with Expiratory Reserve Volume (ERV)

Inhale and exhale one time in tidal volume. At the end of the exhalation, after a short pause, try to breathe out even more. This can be done either by moving the ribs or the belly. Can you feel this?

Maximum ERV while coughing

If you want to explore the most complete volume of ERV, first exhale deeply in ERV.

Now cough seven to ten times, but without taking a breath between the coughs. Feel how far into ERV you can go. There is no real limit.

The more you cough, the more the expiratory muscles will have to work.

ERV in costal breathing

Try to find ERV exhalation by moving the ribs, as shown on page 201.

You can do this in different ways:

- by tightening your ribs as much as possible around the sternum, as if you wanted to close your rib cage from the front

- by lowering your sternum toward the pelvis

- by lowering your ribs toward the sides of the waist.

ERV in abdominal breathing

Try to do ERV exhalation with a movement that makes the abdomen sink inward.

Suck in your stomach above the navel at the mid-trunk (the epigastrium), or contract your abdominals from bottom to top (see detailed description on page 203).

Exhaling in "steps" in ERV

Start by breathing normally in tidal volume.

The next time you exhale, try to breathe out as much air as you can. Then stop breathing for a moment (apnea).

Exhale again and hold your breath.

If you can, exhale another time, and finally release by breathing in.

This method of exhaling in steps helps you develop efficient ERV breathing and to exhale much more than you ever thought possible.

At the end, your expiratory muscles are working powerfully. Be mindful of the tone of your perineum (or lack thereof), because deep exhalations can create strong pressure toward the pelvis.

Apneas in ERV

After several normal breaths, breathe out slowly in a deep ERV, as previously described.

Then remain several seconds in apnea at the end of the ERV. This apnea is not a time of relaxation, but of intense muscular activity. Can you feel the static contraction of the expiratory muscles either in the rib cage or in the abdomen and perineum?

Inhalation in ERV

Repeat the previous exercise and prolong the apnea slightly. Now notice the inhalation that follows:

To inhale again, you must relax all the expiratory muscles that were working so intensely before.

Inhalation in ERV and extension in tidal volume

Repeat the previous exercise.

This time when you inhale, try to let it continue until you've finished a full active inhalation.

There is a moment where the passive inhalation becomes active:

- Immediately after each ERV exhalation, there is a *passive* inhalation: The lungs passively resume their position and shape after being compressed during exhalation.

- This becomes an *active* inhalation when the lungs are opened again using the inspiratory muscles, either the diaphragm or the costal inspiratory muscles.

Try to feel this transition between passive and active inhalation.

The complete breath

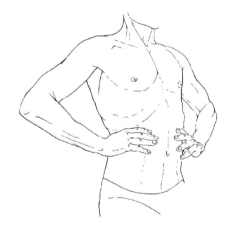

This exercise is taught in a number of traditions. It usually provides a sequence of respiratory movements which affect the three main levels of the trunk. The exercise is first described step by step. This is followed by an explanation, *in italics,* of the respiratory mechanism that accompanies it.

This exercise can be practiced in any position.

First, inhale with a movement that is as low as possible and bulges your abdomen to the front and bottom.

This is a diaphragmatic inhalation (1st mechanism), which affects the lower abdomen.

Now exhale so that the stomach is sucked in at the same location.

This is a low abdominal exhalation via the abdominal muscles (performing a visceral action*) completed by the pelvic floor at the bottom.

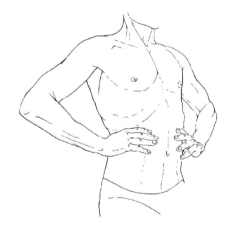
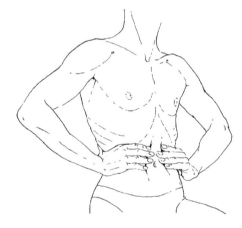

Now inhale by moving the bottom part of the rib cage and the area above the navel.

This is a diaphragmatic inhalation (2nd mechanism), which moves the lower ribs.

Exhale by lowering the sternum and the ribs in the same area.

This is a costal exhalation that is done with the abdominal muscles performing a skeletal action.*

....

*See page 96 for a description of the visceral and skeletal actions of the abdominal muscles.

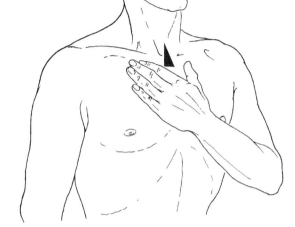

Inhale as deeply as possible by raising the ribs at the top of the thorax.

This is a costal inhalation via the pectoralis minor and major muscles.

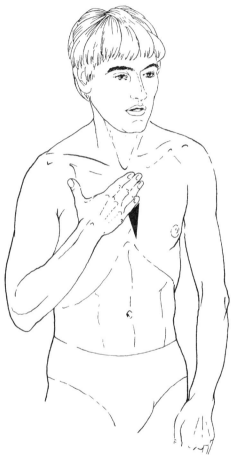

Exhale while moving the same area by lowering the top of the sternum and the top ribs (under the clavicle).

This is an exhalation facilitated by gravity, which causes the ribs to drop, and the transversus thoracis, which closes the rib cage in the front.

Now, do a sequence of these three levels during one inhalation or exhalation:

- *During inhalation,* first make the bottom of the abdomen bulge out. Continue by making the top of the abdomen bulge out, and by opening the lowest ribs. Then finish by raising the rib cage at the top. This is a deep IRV.

- *During exhalation,* first suck in the bottom of the abdomen. Continue by sucking in the portion of the abdomen at rib-level above the navel. Then finish by lowering the top of the sternum.

This deep breathing has the advantage of mobilizing the entire trunk. However, remember that you do not actually breathe into the parts of the body mentioned (the abdomen, epigastrium, etc.) Whatever air you inhale always goes straight to your lungs (see page 22).

211

Sequence of posterior breaths

This section shows a possible sequence of successive breaths, each of which was described in previous chapters. This exercise is performed by two people. One person (A) places his or her hands on different levels of the back of the other person (B), helping B localize breathing movements. These levels correspond to areas, muscles, and mechanisms of different types of breathing.

The goal is for B to perceive the mobility and the posterior breathing in those areas where A's hands are placed, guided by the contact, pressure, and warmth of A's hands. (This exercise can also be practiced by a single person).

Sit on a chair or stool. Put your feet on an object (a small crate, a low stool) to elevate your knees and to keep your hips well flexed and pressed against the abdomen.

Bend forward, with your abdomen resting on your thighs. You may place a cushion under your stomach, or change the height of the object under your feet and the position of your arms, in order to round your spine in forward flexion and to make sure that it is well supported in the front.

1st level

A places her hands at the back of the lower part of B's waist, hands pointing toward the iliac crests, the area generally called "the hips."

A posterior breath at this area corresponds to diaphragmatic breathing (1st mechanism), which presses toward the back and the pelvis.

2nd level

A places her hands at the back of B's waist.

This is still a diaphragmatic breath (1st mechanism), which presses against the back, not so much toward the pelvis, but rather toward the lumbar area.

3rd level

A places her hands at the back of B's waist, but higher, pointing toward the lower edge of the ribs.

This is posterior diaphragmatic breathing (2nd mechanism).

4th level

A places her hands at the back of B's ribs, under the level of the shoulder blade.

This is posterior costal breathing.

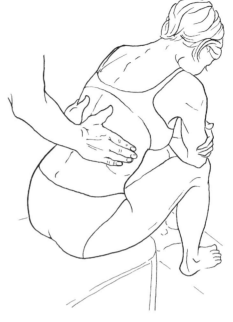

5th level

A places her hands at the back of B's ribs, between the shoulder blades.

This is still costal breathing, but high costal breathing. In this area, there is less movement because the ribs are less mobile at this level.

6th level

A places her hands on top of B's ribs, at the border between the ribs and the bottom of the neck.

This is high posterior costal breathing performed by the serratus posterior superior.

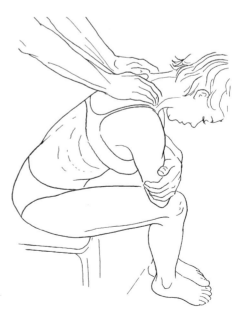

Breathing while staying in IRV

Take a very deep breath in (IRV). Breathe out slightly, without completely emptying your lungs of the inhaled air. Immediately take another breath. Exhale again, but do *not* return to tidal volume expiration by completely breathing out all the inhaled air. Now inhale again.

Repeat this sequence for about ten breathing cycles.

You can pause after the exhalation, but this pause is in IRV.

Can you feel that your inspiratory muscles are always contracted during this type of breathing? This can gradually strengthen them if it is done consciously and voluntarily.

However, if you continue this type of breathing without being aware of it (which happens, e.g., if you are in a stressful situation), this permanent contraction of the inspiratory muscles can cause a tense, exhausting respiration (see "Panting" on page 155).

Lamaze breathing

This type of breathing has been recommended for several decades for use during childbirth. Using all the facts that we have accumulated in the preceding chapters, we can now practice and analyze this type of breathing.

Inhale, still using the same technique as above, resting in IRV, but with an additional detail: Take your breaths as high as possible in the rib cage. This is breathing performed especially by the scalene muscles (see pages 198 and 199).

Exhale a little, and then inhale as quickly as possible. Do not let the movement extend into your lower ribs or abdomen.

Feel how this type of breathing especially mobilizes the top part of the trunk and leaves the lower part practically motionless.

This is recommended for women during childbirth, in order to help them ignore the contractions of the diaphragm and to disassociate the diaphragmatic contractions from the contractions of the uterus.

The problem is that, for a beginner, breathing from the top often causes hyperventilation, which in turn causes stress, which is not useful in childbirth.

Staying in ERV for several breaths

Breathing with opposite forces: passive inhalation — active exhalation

You can do this exercise in any position you like.

Start by exhaling very deeply (in a more or less intense ERV). Feel the expiratory muscles work, either by lowering the ribs or by pushing the abdomen upward. This is an active exhalation.

Now take in a breath, but with little volume. Do not exceed the threshold of tidal volume. Follow up with a quick exhalation while stressing the amplitude of the movement.

This inhalation is passive while the exhalation is active. This is the opposite of what usually happens in tidal volume.

Repeat this routine for several breathing cycles.

Do you recognize what some teachers mean when they say "Let yourself inhale, breathe out with intensity"?

Conclusion

THE INFORMATION PRESENTED in this book is intended to serve as a tool for teaching and practicing the movements of breathing. It can be used in a variety of situations, both professional and in daily life. Examples are provided below. For some of these applications, supplements to this book are being planned.

Movement professionals — ballet dancers, dance teachers, and so forth — may be helped by better harmonizing breathing with the movements of the body that they perform or teach. They can learn how to synchronize gestures where breathing facilitates the movement (e.g., lifting the arms while inhaling) or how to coordinate contradictory movements, which seem to go in the opposite direction from the movement of the body (e.g., lifting the arms while exhaling). This can enrich the movement, making it more accessible at times, or giving it variety or nuance.

Those who practice relaxation techniques may use the rhythms or respiratory volumes to reduce body tension.

For those who work with body awareness, changes in tension in relation to breathing may help to refine the awareness of sensations.

Similarly, those working in the field of mind-body techniques may recognize and adapt with more insight the reciprocal relationships between the emotions and breathing.

Professionals who work with the thorax and abdomen in movement may refine the accuracy of synchronizations (breathing or not breathing) which interfere with the compression-decompression dynamic. I hope to address this topic more fully in a subsequent book on the thorax, abdomen, and abdominal muscles.

Those who do voice work focused on improving or just protecting the voice may try to better harmonize breathing with the voice. This topic too will be explored later in a book on the anatomy of the voice and vocal breathing techniques.

BIBLIOGRAPHY

Basmadjan, P.V. *Anatomie*. Paris: Editions Maloine

Bellugue, P. *Introduction à l'étude de la forme humaine, anatomie plastique et mécanique*. Paris: Editions Maloine

Bouchet/Cuilleret. *Anatomie topographique, descriptive et fonctionnelle*. Villeurbanne: Simep-Editions

Brizon, J., Castaing, J. *Les feuillets d'anatomie*. Paris: Editions Maloine

Campignon, P. *Respir-actions*. ICT GDS

Castaing, J. *Anatomie fonctionnelle de l'appareil locomoteur: Cahier sue le complexe de l'épaule*. Paris: Editions Vigot

Castaing, J., Santini, J.J. *Anatomie fonctionnelle de l'appareil locomoteur: Le rachis*. Paris: Editions Vigot

Clemente, Carmine D. *Anatomy: A Regional Atlas of the Human Body*. Vienna: Urban & Schwarzenberg

Dolto, B. *Le corps entre les mains*. Paris: Editions Flammarion

Kapandji, A. *Physiologie articulaire*. Paris: Editions Maloine

Bibliography

Kendall, Wadsworth. *Les muscles.* Paris: Editions Maloine

McMinn, Hutchings, Logan. *Anatomie de la tête et du cou.* Paris: Editions André Delcourt

Marieb. *Anatomie et physiologie humaines.* Editions De Boeck Université

Netter, Frank H. *Atlas d'anatomie humaine.* Paris: Editions Maloine

Rouviere, H. *Anatomie humaine descriptive et topographique.* Editions Masson

Sobotta. *Atlas d'anatomie.* Paris: Editions Maloine

Wheater, Young, Heath. *Histologie fonctionnelle.* Editions De Boeck Université

INDEX

with bulging belly, 156
of expiratory reserve volume (ERV), 122
force increased by expiratory muscles, 96
holding in IRV, 207
inspiratory actions during, 157
of IRV, 121
lengthening, 178
lungs as primary force of, 11
muscles involved in, 33
rate increased by expiratory muscles, 96
thoracic mechanism of, 146–147
of tidal volume, 119, 140
using to stretch, 169
Expiratory crank motion, 91
Expiratory muscles, 79, 96
　abdominal muscles, 96–97
　concentric work in ERV exhalation, 122
　contraction in laugh mechanism, 156
　external obliques, 99
　inactivity in IRV breathing, 120, 121
　inactivity in tidal volume breathing, 119
　internal obliques, 98
　ischiococcygeus, 101
　levator ani, 101
　pelvic floor muscles, 101
　quadratus lumborum, 103
　rectus abdominis, 100
　relaxation during ERV inhalation, 123
　serratus posterior inferior, 103
　strengthening through ERV exhalation, 122
　transversus abdominis, 97
　transversus thoracis, 102
Expiratory reserve volume (ERV), 28
　alveolar representation, 30
　in costal breathing, 208
　in costal inhalation exercises, 189
　in diaphragm stretching exercise, 173
　exhaling, 122, 140
　experimenting with, 208–209
　forces affecting, 122–123
　increased through expiratory muscles, 96
　increasing amplitude of, 29
　inhaling, 123, 209
　maintaining apnea of, 108
　maximum while coughing, 208
　production by abdominal muscles, 178
　remaining after exhaling tidal volume, 119
　remaining for several breaths, 215
　spirometric representation, 31
External intercostals, 104
External obliques, 99
　in thoracic exhalation, 147
External respiration, 14, 15

F

Female Pelvis, The, 150
Floating ribs, 40
Foramen magnum, 55
Forces
　affecting breathing rate, 124
　affecting respiratory volumes, 117
　in ERV breathing, 122–123
　in ERV breathing, 120–121
　in tidal volume breathing, 118–119
Forward bending
　expiratory direction of, 115
　Valsalva's method for, 151
Frequency of breathing, 32
Frontal bone, 55, 72

G

Gas exchange, in respiration, 15
Gingiva, 74
Glenoid cavity, of scapula, 53
Global anterior diaphragmatic inhalation, 179–181
Global expiratory muscles, 104
Glottal stop, 130
Glottis, 69
　closing and opening during cough mechanism, 154
　closing for abdominal organ decompression, 150
　holding open in diaphragm-stretching exhalation, 173, 174
Gravity, 107
　and costal exhalations, 200
　exhalation facilitated by, 211
Greater pelvis, 51

H

Hard palate, 55, 75
Head
　respiratory organs in, 57
　spinal column support for, 44
Headstand, gravity and diaphragm action in, 113
Heart, diaphragm and, 84
Helping side, breathing into, 169
Hiccupping, 154
High costal breathing, 213
High posterior costal breathing, 213
Higher thoracic articulations, axis of movement, 48
Hip bones, 50
Hip joints, 51
Humerus, 53
Hyaline cartilage tissue, 42
Hyperventilation, 214
　in IRV without physical effort, 206